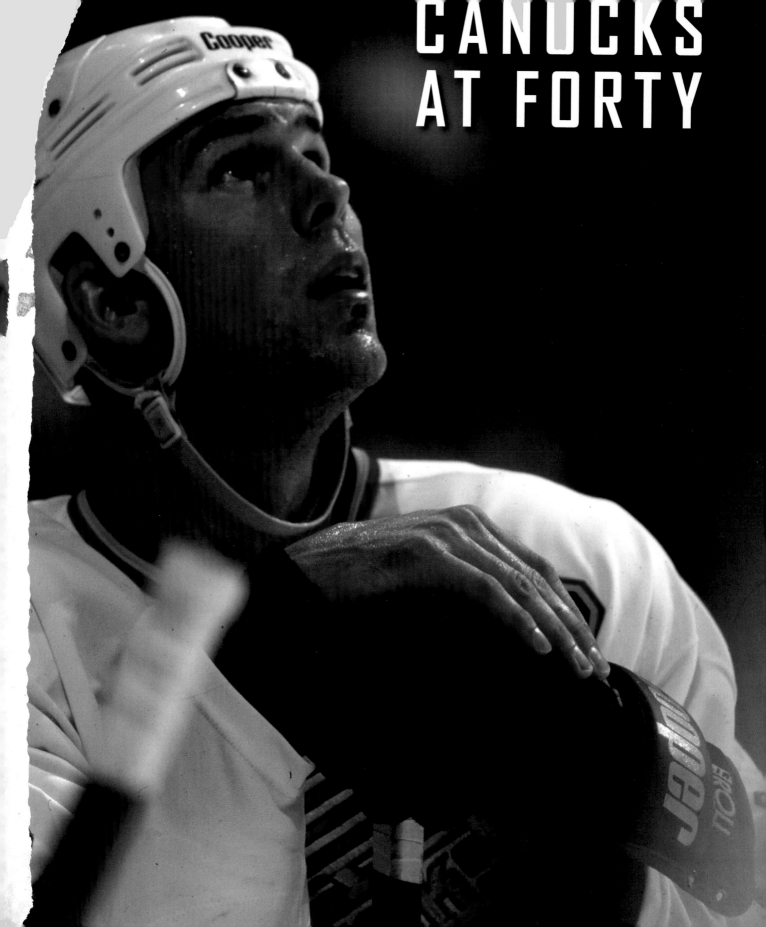

CANUCKS
AT FORTY

GREG DOUGLAS & GRANT KERR

CANUCKS AT FORTY

OUR GAME, OUR STORIES, OUR PASSION

WILEY

John Wiley & Sons Canada, Ltd.

Right: The newly-named ◯ **ROGERS ARENA**, home of the Vancouver Canucks.

Library and Archives Canada Cataloguing in Publication
Douglas, Greg, 1944-
        Canucks at 40 : our game, our stories, our passion / Greg Douglas and Grant Kerr.

ISBN 978-0-470-67916-6

        1. Vancouver Canucks (Hockey team)—History. I. Kerr, Grant II. Title. III. Title: Canucks at forty.

GV848.V35D69 2010   796.962'640971133   C2010-903729-4

Production Credits
Cover design: Adrian So
Interior text design and typesetter: Adrian So
Printer: Friesens

John Wiley & Sons Canada, Ltd.
6045 Freemont Blvd.
Mississauga, Ontario
L5R 4J3

Printed in Canada

1 2 3 4 5 FP 14 13 12 11 10

More than a celebration of 40 years of Vancouver Canucks hockey, this book is a salute to the fans who have helped build this franchise from the ground up. Your dedication and passion will be what puts us over the top.

~ The Vancouver Canucks

To Deirdre, my loving wife and best friend. To my brothers Tom and Norm, and sister Nancy. Also, to Monica and Pierre and two lively grandsons, Kaden and Cole, who are both definite future NHL first-round draft picks.

~ Greg

To Judy, my partner and soul mate. To my sons Scott, Kevin and vvdaughters Taylor and Tessa. And never to be forgotten, my loving mother Annis, always an inspiration to the Kerr family.

~ Grant

CONTENTS

by Jim Robson

FOREWORD

TIME FLIES WHEN YOU'RE HAVING FUN.

I know that for a fact. The 40-year history of the Vancouver Canucks in the National Hockey League has just flown by.

It doesn't seem that long ago that I was studying the 1970–71 National Hockey League schedule to see when the Original Six teams were coming to Vancouver.

In 1970, Gordie Howe was a Detroit Red Wing, Bobby Orr was a Boston Bruin, Jean Beliveau was a Montreal Canadien, Bobby Hull was a Chicago Blackhawk, Rod Gilbert was a New York Ranger and Davey Keon was a Toronto Maple Leaf.

They would all come into the Pacific Coliseum wearing those colourful dark uniforms, as the NHL wisely ruled in those days.

Hockey's finest league had finally admitted a team from Western Canada and fans from Winnipeg west were making plans to attend games in Vancouver. Prior to the fall of 1970, the only way to see NHL stars was to squint at the small TV screens, many still in black and white.

Fans would rush into the Coliseum to see the familiar names on the visiting rosters, but often left the rink buzzing about how tough and competitive the brand new home team was. Who wouldn't be impressed by the character of Orland Kurtenbach and Pat Quinn, or the skill of Andre Boudrias, Bobby Schmautz and Dale Tallon.

Above: Hockey Hall of Fame broadcaster Jim Robson witnessed most of the highlights when it comes to the NHL history of the Vancouver Canucks.

Left: It's a championship moment as Canucks players (left to right) Sergio Momesso, Trevor Linden, Greg Adams, Gerald Diduck and Geoff Courtnall admire the Clarence S. Campbell Bowl presented to the Western Conference winners in 1994 at the Pacific Coliseum.

Those are some of the names you will read about in this special volume, put together by some good friends of mine who know how to tell a story.

They will cover many "eras" of the Canucks' first 40 seasons.

There's the Fox era, when Western Hockey League legend Phil (Fox) Maloney became general

Team captain Markus Naslund accepts congratulations from Ed Jovanovski (55) and Todd Bertuzzi (44) after scoring against Chicago.

manager and head coach, leading the Canucks to their first divisional title and playoff appearance. Sure it was only five games against the mighty Canadiens, but it produced a rare win *in* Montreal, plus a series finale that was a long overtime thriller ending with a fluke goal out of the corner by the brilliant Guy Lafleur.

The mid-1970s also produced a couple of memorable draft picks, a talented Ron Sedlbauer and a tough kid from Edmonton named Harold Snepsts, who became one of the most popular Canucks of all time.

The next era of note was the Jake Milford era, when that wily old hockey man rebuilt the franchise. He brought in interesting coaches such as the colourful Harry Neale and the innovative Roger Neilson. (Remember when they made fun of Roger and called him Captain Video for using something called videotape to study team tendencies and systems?)

Canucks drafting in the Milford area produced character players such as Glen Hanlon, Curt Fraser, Doug Lidster, Garth Butcher and a third-rounder nicknamed "Steamer." Stan Smyl was the heart and soul of the Canucks for his entire 13-year career.

Milford also reached across the Atlantic like no other GM, bringing in several Swedes, including standouts Thomas Gradin, Patrik Sundstrom and Lars Lindgren. And then Jake invaded Czechoslovakia to sign European stars Ivan Hlinka and Jiri Bubla.

There were other off-ice moves that produced Darcy Rota, Ivan Boldirev, Doug Halward, Tiger Williams and a little-known goaltender named

There remains just that one major prize to capture. I'm looking forward to standing on the curb at Georgia and Burrard, watching a Stanley Cup parade.

Richard Brodeur, who became "King" Richard in the surprising run all the way to the 1982 Stanley Cup Final.

The mid-1980s were not all rosy for the Canucks and their fans, but it was still exciting when the line of Tony Tanti, Patrik Sundstrom and Petri Skriko came on the ice. That trio produced 191 goals in two seasons.

But then came the Quinn era. Arthur Griffiths stole Pat Quinn from the Los Angeles Kings to become general manager of the Canucks and survived a court case to keep him. The big Irishman's return to Vancouver meant big changes.

The member of the original Canucks went about building a powerhouse through trades, although he drafted two outstanding Canucks legends. One was a team leader from Medicine Hat, Alberta, and Quinn often called the drafting of Trevor Linden one of his best-ever moves. Trevor's huge army of fans would agree. Then there was a fifth-round gem named Pavel Bure, soon named the Russian Rocket, and the most exciting Canuck

Ownership's Arthur Griffiths (left) celebrates the good times with assistant captain Greg Adams during the 1994 run to the Stanley Cup Final.

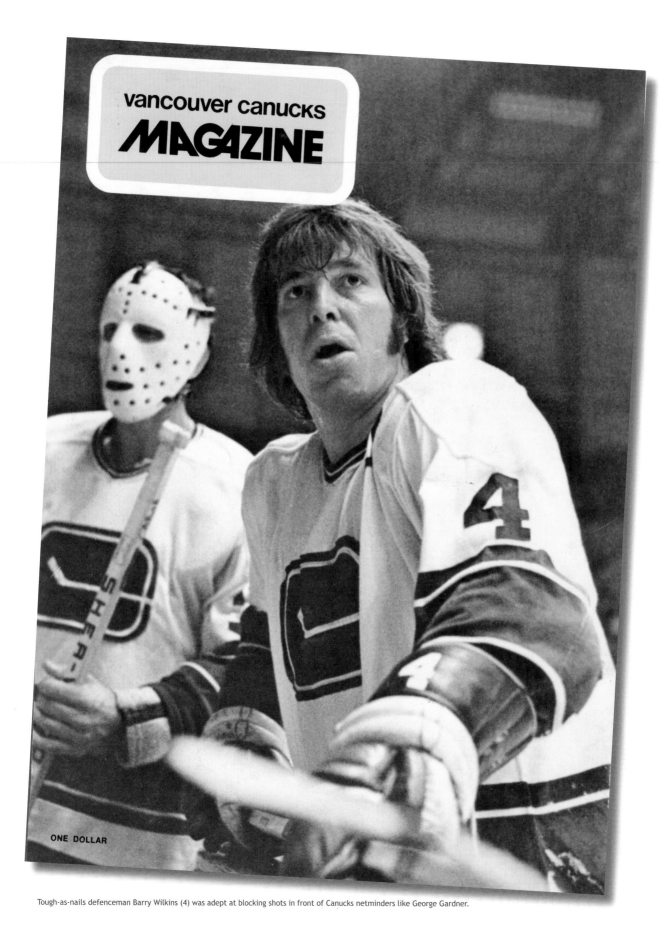

vancouver canucks
MAGAZINE

ONE DOLLAR

Tough-as-nails defenceman Barry Wilkins (4) was adept at blocking shots in front of Canucks netminders like George Gardner.

Canucks fans rise up in joyous celebration of another Vancouver goal as the offence clicks against the Los Angeles Kings.

ever. Many of his 288 Vancouver league and play-off goals are still remembered as highlights in Canucks history.

There was the acquisition of Soviet stars Igor Larionov and Vladimir Krutov, plus all those trades. Quinn dealt for standout goalie Kirk McLean, built his deep defence of Lumme, Murzyn, Babych, Hedican, Brown, Diduck, Dirk and Glynn, and traded for forwards Greg Adams, Cliff Ronning, Geoff Courtnall, Sergio Momesso, Murray Craven and Martin Gelinas. Add tough Gino Odjick to the mix and the Quinn-era Canucks could walk into any rink in the league knowing they had a good chance to win.

This was the team that brought Canucks fans their most memorable moments—the 1994 Stanley Cup playoffs. Fifteen wins, six in overtime and one of the finest Cup Finals ever.

But that 16th win belonged to the New York Rangers, who celebrated their first Stanley Cup in 54 years—which illustrates just how tough it is to win the oldest trophy in professional sports.

Who can forget that scene at the end of Game 7 in Madison Square Garden? There was a battered, bruised, exhausted captain Trevor Linden, on one knee along the boards, trying to cope with that terrible feeling of coming this far without winning the Cup.

So now we have moved into the Gillis era. The Aquilini family surprised the hockey world when they signed Mike Gillis as Canucks president and general manager in August 2009. A hard worker as a player, a respected player agent, but never before a general manager, Mike Gillis set a high target right off the bat. The Canucks hit the 100-point mark in his first season and continued to excite the fans in a sold-out building.

There remains just that one major prize to capture. I'm looking forward to standing on the curb at Georgia and Burrard, watching a Stanley Cup parade. Some old fan will recognize me and say, "Boy, was this a long time coming."

And I'll say, "It wasn't really that long. It just flew by. Time flies when you're having fun."

PREFACE

The rationale behind *Canucks at Forty* was simple: telling you something you don't know.

Whether the Vancouver Canucks have recently caught your eye or you've been along for the ride since 1970, you're surely familiar with the greatest moments in team history.

The spin of a roulette wheel. Our first playoff berth. Playing for the Stanley Cup. Towel Power. Tiger's stick ride. Drafting Captain Canuck and the Russian Rocket. Back-to-back Smythe Division wins. A return to the Cup Final. Heartbreak in New York. General Motors Place. Snagging the Sedins. The West Coast Express. The trade for Luongo. Three Northwest Division titles in five years. An Art Ross and Hart Trophy win.

Compelling stories have shaped the legacy of the Canucks, stories that are etched within us all, stories that unite Canucks fans the world over.

This book is a celebration of 40 years of Canucks hockey and the stories that have captivated us, but never before have they been told like this. Unprecedented access to the team's photo archives and commentary from players and coaches was granted to bring you a behind-the-scenes look at some of your dearest Canucks memories and the characters responsible for them.

Dale Tallon, Vancouver's first ever draft pick, became a Canuck thanks to a numerical twist of fate. Rosaire Paiement, aka *Cracklin' Rosie*, once

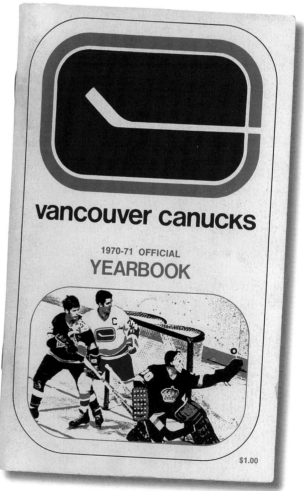

Above: This is where it all began: Orland Kurtenbach tangling with LA's Dale Hoganson as Denis DeJordy makes a glove save on October 9, 1970.

Left: Henrik Sedin (right) is congratulated by twin Daniel after scoring during a game against the Los Angeles Kings in Vancouver on March 13, 2009.

In celebrating 40 years of Canucks hockey we're really paying tribute to you for your loyalty, passion and commitment to the team.

Canucks fans always adore their heroes and 1980s defenceman Colin Campbell obliges this enthusiastic group.

endured a scoring slump that even a hypnotist couldn't bump. Garry Monahan scored one of the most significant goals in franchise history on a one-against-six rush. Or did he?

Greg Adams! Greg Adams! Greg Adams! The Canucks forward's playoff goal, and broadcaster Jim Robson's play-by-play call of it, will go down as one of the greatest one-two combinations ever. Queen Elizabeth II got a red carpet welcome over freshly flooded ice in Vancouver and outperformed many NHL linesmen.

Roberto Luongo, a creature of habit, was out of his routine during Team Canada's golden day at the 2010 Winter Olympics. Henrik Sedin won the Art Ross and Hart Trophies not because he focused on shooting, but because of his attention to detail.

"The Franchise" Glen Hanlon proved the Canucks belonged in the same rink as the storied Montreal Canadiens. Harry Neale still has no idea why Jake Milford selected him to coach in Vancouver.

Ron Delorme's fists were behind one of the most infamous fights in team history and they only let up because of a gentlemen's agreement. John Garrett barely had time to let the paint dry on his mask before being thrust into the NHL All-Star Game.

Trevor Linden got a tearfully rousing sendoff after his final game, but he was crying long before the fans said goodbye. Gino Odjick kept one thing in mind on the only penalty shot attempt of his career: keep it simple, stupid.

This is just a taste of the 40 stories that fill the following pages and although the players, coaches and management take centre stage, it goes without saying that there are no stories, no book, no Canucks as they are today without the fans.

In celebrating 40 years of Canucks hockey we're really paying tribute to you for your loyalty, passion and commitment to the team. Competing in the NHL is a rocky road at the best of times, but your rallying cheers that come when the team needs them most help smooth it out.

You make Canucks hockey unforgettable.

The rationale behind *Canucks at Forty* was simple: telling you something you don't know.

Here we go.

Vancouver supporters are never hesitant to wave their white towels in support of their beloved Canucks.

ACKNOWLEDGEMENTS

Above: Popular Canucks defenceman Harold Snepsts shows a young fan how to hold a hockey stick as part of community involvement.

Left: Young Canucks fans reach out to touch their hero after another three-star salute to Trevor Linden.

If there's one thing missing from *Canucks at Forty*, it's hockey clichés.

But you can't have a hockey book without clichés, so we thought we'd put them all in these acknowledgements.

Project lead Paul Dal Monte put the biscuit in the basket. His efforts, united with those of Mark Raham, Mike Hall and T.C. Carling, aka the hardest working line in hockey, along with Chelsey Perrella, made this book what it is. Every story, every photo and every caption had the tall task of deking through this tight knit unit.

Authors Greg Douglas and Grant Kerr didn't pull any punches in getting to the heart of each story. The talented list of contributors they surrounded themselves with made for a formidable team, one never content to sit on a lead.

Copy-editor Stephanie Maniago and copy-editor/writer Derek Jory brought their A-game and gave 110 per cent.

The big three of Norm Jewison, Jim Robson and Gerry Sillers worked in unison as the historical conscience, standing up factual inaccuracies at the blueline. The collected wealth of knowledge shared between Jewison, Robson and Sillers took care of unforced errors, causing others to make adjustments. You were each an inspiration for this book. You put on a clinic out there.

If a picture is worth a thousand words then Jeff Vinnick and Bill Cunningham did a lot of the heavy lifting thanks to their epic frozen moments. When you put the puck on net, good things happen and this duo always knew when to shoot.

Pacific Newsgroup, Canadian Press and Getty Images came off the bench and really dazzled with their creativity. Each played between the whistles and took it one game at a time.

Towel power became a Vancouver staple in 1982 when the Canucks went to the Stanley Cup Final for the first time. The powerful tradition has never wavered through the decades of NHL hockey in Vancouver.

Without the fans, none of this matters.

John Wiley & Sons Canada, Ltd., and specifically Karen Milner, really came through in the clutch. In gut check time they outlined the x's and o's and ensured the i's were dotted and t's crossed allowing everyone to elevate their game to another level.

Literary agent Robert Mackwood never got beat to loose pucks and proved to be the game changer for a team that really hit its stride and played to its strengths.

We knew what we had to do and went out and did it. It was a total team effort made possible only because of you, the greatest fans in the world.

Without the fans, none of this matters.

—*The Vancouver Canucks*

The authors would like to thank the many hockey personalities who responded to our queries about the first 40 years of Vancouver Canucks history. We were received warmly and appreciate the thoughtful insights that we were allowed to share in our story telling.

A special thanks goes to our contributors who were approached to enhance this project. They are, in alphabetical order: Jim Hughson, *Hockey Night in Canada* play-by-play broadcaster;

Norm Jewison, long-time Canucks publicist; Ben Kuzma, *Vancouver Province* hockey journalist; Iain MacIntyre, *Vancouver Sun* sports columnist; Elliott Pap, *Vancouver Sun* hockey journalist; Garry Raible, Vancouver sports broadcaster; Don Taylor, Pacific Region Sportsnet host.

We would be remiss not to recognize Hockey Hall of Fame broadcaster Jim Robson, Vancouver's own walking hockey encyclopedia.

—*Grant and Greg*

Rogers Arena (formerly General Motors Place) opened in 1995 and provides hockey fans with incredible sight lines to view their favourite Canucks players in action.

OCTOBER 9, 1970
Historic hockey night in Vancouver

AS FAR AS THE NATIONAL TELEVISION audience tuned in to a special Friday night edition of *Hockey Night in Canada* was concerned, everything was going according to plan on October 9, 1970.

That was the historic night when Vancouver was officially welcomed to the National Hockey League, with the Canucks making their debut at the Pacific Coliseum against the Los Angeles Kings.

All appeared orderly and remarkably organized as Premier W.A.C. Bennett accompanied league president Clarence Campbell and Vancouver mayor Tom Campbell to centre ice, with the British Columbia Beefeater Band trumpeting the dignitaries' red carpet arrival.

But behind the scenes? Not so orderly and not so remarkably organized, at least in the life of Norman Robert (Bud) Poile, the Canucks' general manager. Juggling last-minute ticket requests and outrageous opening night favours from "friends" he hadn't heard from in years, Poile was desperately trying to escape from his office and join the official party in the board room where several NHL owners and governors had gathered.

As he stepped into the main lobby from his private quarters, Poile ran smack into Howie Young, who'd been waiting for his GM. "Why aren't I dressing tonight?" Young shouted in a loud and obnoxious voice. "I'm the most experienced defenceman you've got on the roster and you're

Above: Highest-priced Canucks seats on opening night at the Pacific Coliseum were $6.50 for the NHL opener against the Los Angeles Kings.

Left: The elusive Stanley Cup is admired in 1970 by Canuck players (left to right) George Gardner, Rosaire Paiement, Ray Cullen and Pat Quinn.

allowing the coach to sit me out on opening night! What the hell's going on?"

Young had spent seven seasons in the NHL bouncing between the Detroit Red Wings and Chicago Blackhawks. Handsome and charismatic, but undisciplined on and off the ice, he had somehow found his way to the Los Angeles Blades of the Western Hockey League.

That's when Hollywood discovered him, resulting in an appearance in the 1965 war movie *None But the Brave*, starring Frank Sinatra.

Young was at the end of his hockey-playing days when Chicago transferred his rights to the expansion Canucks, who were willing to take any potential help they could get.

Poile settled Young down with the promise he'd be suiting up against the Toronto Maple Leafs two nights later. It would be one of 11 starts with Vancouver before Young was released.

Poile again pointed himself in the direction of the board room. In his path stood Chief Dan George, a proud member of the Coast Salish Nation who'd been invited as a special guest to take part in the opening night festivities. "Mr. Poile, I don't have credentials or a ticket to get into the game," the chief said. "Your switchboard lady asked me if I had a reservation. I told her, 'Of course … the Burrard Reservation in North Vancouver where my people have been for years.' But she still won't let me into the building!"

Chief Dan George was also a movie star, having just completed the 1970 film *Little Big Man* with a young Dustin Hoffman.

Poile shook his head, rolled his eyes and apologized to the chief, inviting him to the board room for a shot of Scotch whisky.

Otherwise, the rest of the evening went well. Canada's singing sweetheart of the time, "Our Pet" Juliette, sang the national anthem, Mayor Campbell was lustily booed, Vancouver-born referee Lloyd Gilmour dropped the puck to get the game underway at 8:22 PDT and defenceman Barry Wilkins scored the Canucks' first-ever goal at 2:14 of the third period.

Jim Robson worked the *Hockey Night in Canada* play-by-play assignment with veteran Toronto broadcaster Jack Dennett as his colour commentator, while local talent Ted Reynolds, Bill Good, Jr., and Babe Pratt hosted the intermissions.

Montreal's Danny Gallivan called the game on radio with CKNW's Al Davidson working as his colour man. It was all a very strange combination of eastern and western broadcasters playing musical chairs, but it worked.

The only downside of the evening for the partisan sellout crowd was a 3–1 opening night loss.

The Canucks line up for a face-off in the Los Angeles zone during the first NHL regular-season game at the Pacific Coliseum as the anxious crowd anticipates Vancouver's first goal.

DALE TALLON
Wheel of misfortune

DALE TALLON'S FATHER WANTED him to be a professional hockey player; his mother thought a hockey and golf scholarship at a U.S. college made more sense.

So, being the polite and well-behaved kid that he was, growing up in Noranda, Quebec, Dale satisfied each of his parents by eventually making a living in both sports.

"I wasn't sure where my career was heading but I knew I wasn't going to stay home," Tallon said in a 1971 magazine profile. "There wasn't much to do in Noranda but work in the mines and drink beer with the boys at the end of your shift. It's a great place for a kid, though. It's winter 10 months of the year and during the short summers I would shoot 54 holes of golf every day."

He left the family nest as a 16-year-old to play his first year of junior hockey in Oshawa and quickly learned what pressure was all about. Tallon, a big-for-his-age defenceman, was billed as the Oshawa Generals' next Bobby Orr, who had just signed with the Boston Bruins. "I had a lousy rookie year," Tallon recalls. "I was forcing everything and nothing was working right."

The following season he was traded to the Toronto Marlies in exchange for five players. "More pressure," he says. "I figured in the eyes of the fans that I had to take the place of five players and again I was forcing things. In my last

Above: Vancouver's first-ever entry draft pick knew as a 16-year-old that he would pursue a pro career.

Left: Dale Tallon's boyish good looks made him an instant hit with fans at the Pacific Coliseum.

year of junior I finally relaxed and it all came together."

If Tallon thought he was under pressure in Oshawa and Toronto, then joining the Vancouver Canucks in 1970 as their first-ever top amateur draft pick must have hit him with all the force of a raging West Coast storm.

It remains in the NHL archives as one of the most bizarre developments in the history of the league.

Tallon (9) and defensive partner Barry Wilkins come to the aid of goaltender Dunc Wilson, with all eyes following the bouncing puck.

With Vancouver and Buffalo having been awarded expansion franchises, NHL president Clarence Campbell decreed that the spin of a roulette wheel would determine which new team would have first choice in what was officially referred to as the 1970 Entry Draft.

The Canucks were allotted numbers one through 10 on the wheel, while the Sabres had 11 through 20. A deafening hush fell over the Grand Salon at the Queen Elizabeth Hotel in Montreal on June 11, 1970, when the wheel stopped spinning and a nervous Campbell announced: "The number is one! Vancouver gets first pick!"

The Canucks delegation, under the direction of general manager Bud Poile, collectively leapt to their feet, clapping and patting each other on the back.

While he was out of hockey he was a head professional at Highland Park Country Club in Chicago and the Tamarack Golf Club in Naperville, Illinois.

There wasn't a hockey man in the room who hadn't rated a dashing young centre by the name of Gilbert Perreault from the Montreal Junior Canadiens as the finest junior prospect on the planet. He had just completed a superb 51-goal and 71-assist season in leading the Junior Habs to their second consecutive Memorial Cup. And now he was about to become property of the Vancouver Canucks.

Or so it seemed.

Above all the commotion was the frantic and demanding voice of George (Punch) Imlach, general manager of the Sabres, on his feet screaming:

"Mr. Campbell … Mr. Campbell … that is not a 'one.' It is an 'eleven.' The digits are one on top of the other!"

There was no denying that Imlach was correct. As a result, Perreault wore jersey No. 11 throughout a spectacular 17-year career that ended with an accumulation of 512 goals and 814 assists in 1,191 games—all with the Sabres. He was named rookie of the year in 1970–71 and was chosen to play in nine All Star Games before his retirement in 1986. In 1990 Perreault was inducted into the Hockey Hall of Fame.

Tallon, meanwhile, on that fateful day in 1970, was chosen by the Canucks as a runner-up pick to Perreault. The 19-year-old youngster had no idea what he would face upon his arrival in Vancouver. It was like the fans were blaming Tallon for the infamous "Wheel of Misfortune."

Despite scoring 46 goals over three seasons and representing the Canucks in two All Star Games, Tallon's days were numbered in Vancouver. He was traded to the Chicago Blackhawks for Gary Smith and Jerry Korab in 1973.

Even his start in Chicago was rocky when the Hawks gave him jersey No. 9 in training camp, the number that had belonged to the fans' favourite, Bobby Hull. After one pre-season game at Chicago Stadium when Tallon was being lustily booed by the Hull faithful, he switched to No. 19. After four uneventful seasons with the Hawks, Tallon was traded to Pittsburgh and that's where he finished his playing career in 1979–80.

A Canadian junior golf champion in 1969, Tallon qualified for the Canadian Tour in 1971. While he was out of hockey he was a head professional at Highland Park Country Club in Chicago and the Tamarack Golf Club in Naperville, Illinois.

Tallon resurfaced in the NHL as a radio and television commentator with the Blackhawks in 1982–83 and was named general manager of the team in the summer of 2005, after working as an assistant under Bob Pulford for two years. Tallon was demoted to senior advisor when the Hawks promoted Stan Bowman, son of Scotty, to the position of general manager in June 2009. His career took yet another turn when he was named General Manager of the Florida Panthers in May, 2010.

Tallon told *Vancouver Sun* columnist Cam Cole during his last trip to Vancouver in April 2009: "I will always have a fondness for this city. I have great memories of Orland Kurtenbach, Pat Quinn and Dennis Kearns and all the guys who taught me a lot about life. I never wanted to leave Vancouver but it didn't work out, so we move on."

It was as though his career with the Canucks was doomed from that infamous June day in 1970 when number one became number 11 and Dale Tallon became number two.

ORLAND KURTENBACH
Original Canucks captain set some "firsts"

Above: An NHL Canuck and first team captain, Vancouver-selected the veteran Kurtenbach in the expansion draft of June 10, 1970.

Left: Orland Kurtenbach's first stop in Vancouver was with the WHL Canucks as a teenager prior to his NHL debut with the New York Rangers in 1960.

DEFENCEMAN BARRY WILKINS will forever be remembered in Vancouver hockey history for scoring the Canucks' first NHL goal in their season opener on October 9, 1970, a Friday night. Despite losing 3-1 to the Los Angeles Kings, Wilkins' goal at 2:14 of the third period against goaltender Denis Dejordy had a sell-out Pacific Coliseum crowd of 15,542 standing as one and craving more of the same.

They didn't have to wait long. The Canucks' second game in that initial year came along less than 48 hours later and the atmosphere was electric in the Coliseum for a Sunday matinee visit from the legendary Toronto Maple Leafs.

Canucks captain Orland Kurtenbach brought the crowd to their feet when he opened the scoring with Vancouver's second goal in the history of the franchise at 13:57 of the opening period. It was also the team's first-ever shorthanded goal and led to the Canucks' first-ever victory in the newly expanded NHL.

"I'll never forget it," Kurtenbach says. "I was trying to pass the puck to Andre Boudrias when (Toronto goaltender) Bruce Gamble intercepted it but also lost control of it. I wound up looking at a wide open net and scored on the backhand. The fact we were killing a penalty sent the crowd into a frenzy."

It was a celebration that extended long into the night as the Canucks proceeded to defeat the hallowed Maple Leafs 5-3.

To this day, Kurtenbach is at a loss to explain how he suddenly became a scoring threat with the Canucks, setting personal season highs of 21 and 24 goals after previous NHL stops with the New York Rangers, the Boston Bruins and the Maple Leafs as a checking centre.

"It didn't make a whole lot of sense, me scoring goals," he says. "I guess I was getting more ice time than before, working the power play and

"I've always felt hockey is a game of tremendous skill and while you were always taught to stand up for your teammates, I never went looking for a fight."

killing penalties . . . things I was rarely asked to do earlier in my career. Also, I wasn't put in the role of being the team's tough guy. We had other players in those early Canucks years who could mix it up: Bobby Schmautz, Rosaire Paiement and Pat Quinn, of course. We stood up to the tough teams of that era."

Quinn, Vancouver's fourth pick in the 1970 Expansion Draft, behind Gary Doak, Kurtenbach and Ray Cullen, says: "We had a cast of characters in those early years but also character guys and Orland was the king of the castle. He put the team first and always protected his teammates. Kurt certainly was our best player and in his role of the team 'policeman,' he became our instant leader."

Kurtenbach says that while he might have established himself as one of the NHL's reigning heavyweight champs of the 1960s, he was never comfortable with that reputation.

"I thought it was demeaning," he says. "I've always felt hockey is a game of tremendous skill and while you were always taught to stand up for your teammates, I never went looking for a fight. Take a look at my career stats. I never served more than 100 penalty minutes in any one season in the NHL."

Born on a farm in Cudworth, Saskatchewan, as the youngest of nine children, Kurtenbach learned early in life the importance of fending for himself. He maintains that some of his historic NHL exchanges with the likes of Elmer (Moose) Vasko, Ted Harris and Terry Harper were the result of simply defending his turf.

"I got into some scraps but nothing was ever premeditated. When it happens, it happens," Kurtenbach says. "I remember one time in Detroit when I was with the Bruins I got reefed from

The Saskatchewan-raised Kurtenbach learned to play with a certain edge that later was beneficial in the NHL when he took on the league's heavyweights.

Kurt and wife Laurel settled in the Vancouver area after his playing and coaching days. They stay busy with family functions that include 18 grandchildren.

behind and was slammed head first into the Red Wings players' bench. I didn't realize it was Gordie Howe who'd hit me. I went after him with my stick but with just a couple of minutes left in the game and Detroit up by a goal, he wasn't interested. That's how smart he was."

When Kurtenbach was taken by the Canucks in the 1970 expansion draft, it would mark his return to Vancouver. As property of the Rangers coming out of his teens, he played for the Western League Canucks in 1957-58 and made his NHL debut in New York two years later.

It was during those early years in Vancouver when Kurtenbach met and fell in love with a Trans Canada Airlines flight attendant. Today Orland and Laurel are the proud parents of six children and have 18 grandchildren: "Just enough for two softball teams," Kurtenbach jokes.

A couple of knee-crunching, low body checks from Toronto's Bobby Baun and Oakland's Hilliard Graves prompted Kurtenbach to retire after the 1973-74 season, especially when it was suggested by the Canucks team doctor that he'd be facing a knee replacement at the age of 45 if he continued playing.

Kurtenbach launched a coaching career with the Canucks-affiliated Seattle Totems in 1974-75 and worked behind the Tulsa Oilers bench for two years (coach-of-the-year in '75-76) before returning to Vancouver for a third time in his career as head coach of the Canucks, taking over from Phil Maloney midway through the '76-77 season. His coaching record in Vancouver was 36-62-27 before being replaced by Harry Neale in 1978.

With family roots well established in the Lower Mainland, Kurtenbach became involved in the British Columbia Hockey League (BCHL), first as a coach with the Richmond Sockeyes and later as a goodwill ambassador under league president and former Canucks defenceman John Grisdale.

"I was proud to be named the first captain of the Vancouver Canucks and I'm proud to be an active member today of the Canucks Alumni," the 74-year-old Kurtenbach says. "Sure, it would have been great to win a few more games for the fans in the early 1970s. But they loved us for what we were and we loved them back. The fond memories will live forever."

Hockey fans throughout British Columbia clearly haven't forgotten what Kurtenbach means to the Canucks organization. He still draws huge crowds wherever he travels representing the Alumni.

"I played two seasons with him but really got to know him after our playing careers were over," says Pat Quinn. "He is a very kind and caring man . . . the type of person everybody would want as a friend."

WAYNE MAKI
Boyhood dream ended far too soon

WAYNE MAKI FULFILLED his boyhood dream when he suited up alongside his older brother Chico with the Chicago Blackhawks during the 1967–68 NHL season.

As kids growing up on the tough side of the tracks in Sault Ste. Marie, Ontario, the Maki boys knew their only ticket out of the steel town would be through professional hockey careers.

While Chico survived 14 seasons in the NHL— all with Chicago—Wayne's journey was much less comfortable and far too brief.

After being claimed from the Blackhawks by St. Louis in the summer of 1969, Maki found himself in the centre of a gruesome stick-swinging controversy that involved Boston Bruins defence-man Ted Green. It happened in a pre-season game in Ottawa on September 21, 1969. They engaged in an ugly exchange of lumber that resulted in Green suffering a fractured skull and brain damage.

Maki was banished to the minors and didn't return to the NHL until the Canucks plucked him from the Blues in the 1970 expansion draft.

Playing left wing on a line with Orland Kurtenbach at centre and Murray Hall on the right side, Maki became an instant hit with fans in Vancouver when he scored two goals in the Canucks' first-ever win: 5–3 over the legendary Toronto Maple Leafs at the Pacific Coliseum on Sunday, October 11, 1970.

Above: Maki yearned to follow in the footsteps of his older brother Chico, a Chicago Blackhawks regular.

Left: A familiar spot for spunky left-winger Wayne Maki, always on the opposition's doorstep as a scoring threat.

Wayne Maki had no fear about driving the net as he boldly attempts to score against the Detroit Red Wings.

"I was never able to explain why the three of us clicked so well in that first year," Kurtenbach said in later years. "The match-up really didn't make sense . . . an old guy like me with a young kid and a journeyman. But it worked. We were all 20-goal scorers."

Maki, in fact, finished second in scoring with 25 goals and 38 assists, just three points behind team leader Andre Boudrias. Kurtenbach and Hall each scored 21 goals.

"What most people didn't know was that Wayne had a hearing problem and couldn't hear out of his right ear," Kurtenbach recalled. "With Wayne playing left wing, it made it difficult for us to communicate. He would have to turn and almost face me in order to hear me. But we got through it."

Kurtenbach said in later years, "The match-up really didn't make sense . . . an old guy like me with a young kid and a journeyman. But it worked. We were all 20-goal scorers."

They also got through the Canucks' first visit to the Boston Garden during that initial season. "I figured Wayne would be a marked man," Kurtenbach, a noted heavyweight contender throughout his NHL career, said. "I had played in Boston and knew how tough those fans can be. It was the first time they would see Wayne in person since the Green incident. Quite frankly, I was a little worried about him, but I told him to stick close to me if there was any trouble. We had some tough guys on our team and while the Bruins kept running at Wayne, nothing serious broke out."

Maki scored 22 goals in his second season with the Canucks and it appeared he had found a happy hockey home in Vancouver with his wife, Bev, and two young children. But on December 10, 1972, Maki underwent emergency surgery for the removal of a brain tumour. He passed away on May 1, 1974, at the alarmingly young age of 29.

ROSAIRE PAIEMENT
Popularity bubbles with "Cracklin' Rosie"

FOR A PLAYER WHO SPENT just two seasons with the infant Vancouver Canucks, from 1970 through 1972, Rosaire Paiement created enough of a stir to be remembered through the years as one of the all-time favourites in club history.

One of 16 children born to a former Canadian senior arm-wrestling champion, he learned early in life about survival. "We had to fend for ourselves," he says while recalling his youth in a tiny farming hamlet in Earlton, Ontario. "If you got to the table late for dinner, odds are you'd go hungry."

Rosaire and Wilf, his younger brother by 10 years, parlayed their tough upbringing into professional hockey careers.

The Canucks' first general manager, Bud Poile, had been watching Rosaire's progress in the Philadelphia Flyers organization and was particularly impressed with the rugged right winger's stats during the 1969–70 season in the American League with the Quebec Aces. Paiement scored 28 goals despite having served 242 minutes in penalties.

Poile wasted no time in selecting Rosaire in Vancouver's 1970 expansion draft.

"I never considered myself to be a big goal-scorer," Paiement says. "I always figured I'd get my 20 and protect my teammates the rest of the time."

He quickly became "Cracklin' Rosie" in the eyes of Canucks fans when he went on a scoring binge in 1970–71, finishing with a team-leading 34 goals. Within an eight-day span in February, Rosaire set club records by becoming the first Canuck to score four goals in a game (on February 9 vs. Buffalo) and the first to collect five points in a game (February 16) with three goals and two

Above: Paiement had impressive scoring numbers in the minors that caught the attention of Canucks management.

Left: Swashbuckling Rosaire Paiement went on a remarkable scoring spree to lead the first Canucks NHL team in goals with 34.

assists in a stirring 5–4 victory against the defending Stanley Cup champion Boston Bruins. He completed his hat trick during the final minute of play, sending a sold-out Pacific Coliseum crowd into a frenzy.

But alas, the crackle in Rosie's scoring flask went flat the following season. After 33 games without a goal and with the fans voicing their dissatisfaction, Paiement became the first—and only—player in Canucks history to agree to seek the assistance of a hypnotist. Columnist Clancy Loranger described the public relations set-up in the *Vancouver Province* on February 2, 1972: "The long goal-scoring drought is about to end for Rosaire Paiement. When the Canucks take to the ice tonight in Oakland, Rosie will be without nervous tension, his reflexes will be sharper than he's ever known possible, his reactions will be split-second perfect and he will score, score, score.

"Who says so? Peter Reveen says so, that's who. Reveen is the world-famous hypnotist and illusionist who worked his wonders on Paiement's subconscious at a press conference in the Hotel Georgia lobby. Paiement was a willing subject. 'Why not?' Rosie said. 'Nothing else is working.'"

As the records show, Paiement failed to score in Oakland. Nor did he break the slump in ensuing games against Chicago, Montreal, and Philadelphia. The drought finally ended in a demoralizing 9–1 loss in Boston on February 10.

Paiement finished the season with just 10 goals but, in his defence, he suffered a severe eye injury in mid-December after being hit by an errant puck from the stick of teammate Dennis Kearns. At one point it was feared Paiement might permanently lose the vision in his left eye.

Unable to agree to terms for a new contract with the Canucks, Paiement extended his playing career for another six seasons in the WHA with Chicago, New England and Indianapolis. He retired during the 1977–78 season after a scuffle with Dave Semenko that resulted in Paiement damaging his eye again.

"Cracklin' Rosie" took up residence in Tamarac, Florida, where he became part-owner of a popular sports bar.

Surrounded by Minnesota North Stars, the intense Paiement thrived when he was in the middle of the action.

JIM ROBSON
Voice of the Canucks over three decades

OF ALL THE FLATTERING WORDS directed at Hall of Fame broadcaster Jim Robson, it is doubtful any can match those penned by the late and legendary Jim Coleman in a *Vancouver Province* column published in November 1992.

"He is an enduring symbol of excellence in sports broadcasting," Coleman wrote. "People who have been listening to his play-by-play description of the Vancouver Canucks marvel at the consistent high quality of his performances. He is the archetypical professional."

Over a career that spanned 29 years covering the Canucks on CKNW Radio and CBC Television, Robson was to Vancouver hockey fans what Foster Hewitt was to the Toronto Maple Leafs and Danny Gallivan to the Montreal Canadiens.

"As a youngster growing up in Western Canada, listening to Foster Hewitt and then Danny Gallivan, in my wildest dreams it never occurred to me that I would get the opportunity to broadcast NHL games," Robson says. "When the chance came along, I never thought I'd end up with the honour of being inducted into the Hockey Hall of Fame."

Not to mention the British Columbia Sports Hall of Fame, the B.C. Hockey Hall of Fame and the Canadian Association of Broadcasters Hall of Fame.

The Robson family moved from Prince Albert, Saskatchewan, to Maple Ridge, British Columbia,

Above: Robson prepared for games just as meticulously as the players during his long tenure with the Canucks, which led him to induction into the Hockey Hall of Fame.

Left: A couple of smiling hockey broadcasters, Jim Robson (right) and Kelly Moore, take a break prior to a Canucks exhibition game.

when Jim was eight years old. As a teenager, his grade 11 Maple Ridge Secondary School class toured CKNW on a professional day and Robson says he knew from that moment on that his future would be in radio.

Jim Robson (left) and John Shorthouse represented different play-by-play eras when they appeared together for a Canucks open house for season ticket holders.

Ironically, the man who would eventually have a hand in hiring him as the Canucks' play-by-play man in 1970 was the same Bill Hughes who had hosted the Maple Ridge students almost 20 years earlier. It was Hughes who had given the skinny redhead named Robson a contact name at CJAV in Port Alberni, where he landed his first job in broadcasting at $100 a month.

Robson's initial taste of play-by-play came with the Alberni Athletics basketball team, and three years later he was broadcasting the 1955 Mann Cup lacrosse finals for the Nanaimo Timbermen on CHUB Radio.

In 1956, the "big time" came calling when Robson was offered a job in Vancouver by CKWX sports director Bill Stephenson. "I asked for $300

The grand old CBC television gang with *Hockey Night in Canada*: from left to right, Jim Robson, Howie Meeker, Walter (Babe) Pratt, Ted Reynolds and Steve Armitage.

a month and when I didn't hear back, I thought I had priced myself out of the market," Robson recalls. And then the magic phone call came.

He was hired as Stephenson's back-up man at a time when CKWX owned the broadcasting rights to the BC Lions, Western Hockey League Vancouver Canucks and Vancouver Mounties of the Pacific Coast Baseball League.

Stephenson moved to Toronto in the early 1960s, leaving Robson to work 18-hour shifts. Robson would announce the daily sportscasts from early morning to the dinner hour, then hustle off to do play-by-play. More times than not, the post-game shows would run until midnight.

Former *Vancouver Sun* columnist Archie McDonald, a B.C. Sports Hall of Fame media member himself, once wrote: "If there was a hall of fame for sports broadcasters' wives, Bea Robson would be a charter inductee. She is a gracious lady, not much interested in sports, which makes for a happily balanced relationship."

In the same article, McDonald related how Jim drove a pregnant Bea to the hospital in July 1958, then headed straight for Capilano Stadium, where the Mounties and the Phoenix Giants were engaged in a heated battle for first place.

"When Mounties' catcher Charlie White hit a home run in the bottom of the ninth for a 4–3 Vancouver win," McDonald wrote, "Robson did his post-game wrap and headed back to the hospital to meet his new daughter, Jennifer, the first of four children. Years later Jennifer would say,: 'You remember the score of the game, but I bet you don't remember my weight when I was born.'"

Colour commentator Garry Monahan (left) worked with Jim Robson in the Canucks radio broadcast booth following Monahan's retirement as a player.

When CKNW landed the broadcast rights for Vancouver's NHL expansion team in 1970, Robson was the automatic choice to be hired as the play-by-play announcer, following a dozen years calling the WHL Canucks on CKWX.

He was the "Voice of the Canucks" for nearly three decades, broadcasting more than 2,000 NHL games on radio and television between 1970 and his retirement in 1999. As part of his 15-year relationship with CBC Television, Robson called three

Stanley Cup Finals for *Hockey Night in Canada* and five NHL All Star Games.

In a gesture to acknowledge Robson's accomplishments, the Griffiths family and John McCaw—then owners of the Canucks—named the announcer's booth at General Motors Place "The Jim Robson Broadcast Gondola."

More than a decade after passing the Canucks' broadcasting torch to Jim Hughson, who, in turn, passed it on to John Shorthouse, Robson is like a

Jim Robson's office at the Pacific Coliseum in the 1970s was high above ice level where he began an NHL broadcasting career that spanned three decades.

He was the "Voice of the Canucks" for nearly three decades, broadcasting more than 2,000 NHL games.

Pied Piper as he negotiates his way through the crowds on game nights.

People young and old reach out to him, expressing their gratitude for his years of sharing his splendid coverage on radio and television.

Embarrassed by the constant affection, Robson thanks the fans for thanking him.

Having celebrated his 75th birthday in January 2010, Jim settled into a comfortable lifestyle with Bea in a trendy Kitsilano home that has become family headquarters for their four grown-up children: Jennifer, Rob, Mike and Stefani, plus grandson Theo—and Daisy the wonder dog.

"Bea and I now spend our days enjoying time with our family and exploring this great province and country," Robson says. "My place in hockey is a small one. It is the owners, general managers, coaches, officials, players and above all, the fans, who are to be celebrated."

Which brings us back to that 1992 column where Coleman concluded: "In a branch of the news media that has been known to foster some enormous egos, Jim Robson is refreshingly diffident and gentlemanly.

"Vancouver—all of British Columbia—should be proud of him."

BOBBY SCHMAUTZ
Goals suddenly came in bunches

A SLIGHT BUT FEISTY RIGHT WINGER who never weighed more than 175 pounds went on a goal-scoring spree for the Vancouver Canucks that had the NHL buzzing during the 1972-73 season.

They were coming in bunches for Bobby Schmautz, beginning with his first-ever NHL hat trick on November 17, and followed by four-goal performances on November 19 and December 30.

"I took too many hits without wearing a helmet to remember how it all shook down," Schmautz jokes. "I do recall getting plenty of ice time from (head coach) Vic Stasiuk and playing with confidence helped a lot. I had been shuffled back and forth from the NHL to the minors and my career was touch and go."

Schmautz led the Canucks in scoring that year, finishing with 38 goals and 33 assists, one point better than linemate Andre Boudrias. Schmautz also led the team in penalty minutes, with 137.

"At my size," Schmautz says, "I had to be tough to survive." His epic scraps with the likes of Dave (Hammer) Schultz, Andre (Moose) Dupont and noted tough guy Dennis Hextall became legendary. But his sudden goal-scoring prowess in Vancouver's third year in the league upstaged his fisticuffs.

"My mom was at the Pacific Coliseum visiting from Saskatoon the night I got the hat trick against Los Angeles," Schmautz remembers. "She said to

Above: Don't let the smile fool you. Schmautz was more than feisty as he'd drop the gloves or use the stick at the bat of an eye, if he wasn't too busy scoring goals.

Left: A sudden two-game, goal-scoring spree by Schmautz created a flurry of publicity for the NHL during the 1972-73 season.

me later: 'Well, you scored three ... why not go for four the next game.' That was two nights later and I'll be darned, I scored four against Buffalo. We went out to Hy's Encore for dinner that night and Mr. Aisenstat, the owner and a great hockey fan, treated us royally. We stayed so late we had to take the service elevator because everything else was shut down."

A typical goalmouth scene for the Canucks: Schmautz in the middle of the action against the Winnipeg Jets late in his career.

There were three hockey-playing Schmautz boys raising Cain in Saskatoon. Arnie was a Western League star during the days of Guyle Fielder, Phil Maloney, and Art Jones, and Cliff played briefly in the NHL with Philadelphia and Buffalo.

Bobby was a goal-scoring machine in his junior days with the Saskatoon Quakers, who later became the Blades. In his final year of junior, he scored 45 goals in 44 games.

The Canucks elevated him from Seattle in 1970-71. Schmautz remained in Vancouver until midway through the 1973-74 season, when he was traded to the Boston Bruins for Fred O'Donnell (who never showed), Chris Oddleifson and the NHL rights to Mike Walton.

"I was driving home and heard about it on my car radio," Schmautz says. "At the time I had been thinking of jumping to the World Hockey Association. There was an offer on the table from Jimmy Pattison's Vancouver Blazers. My agent (North Vancouver lawyer Ron Perrick) advised me to go to Boston. Boy, was that good advice."

Schmautz enjoyed seven productive seasons with the Bruins and, ironically, his NHL career wound down in Vancouver in 1980-81.

"For a skinny kid from Saskatoon who was never supposed to make it," Schmautz says, "I did okay."

Gerry Sillers, president of the Canucks Alumni, grew up with the Schmautz brothers and

"She said to me later: 'Well, you scored three . . . why not go for four the next game.' That was two nights later and I'll be darned, I scored four against Buffalo."

was Bobby's teammate with the junior Saskatoon Blades. "Pound for pound, he was as tough as they got," Sillers says. "Bobby liked to sing songs and tell jokes on the team bus but once it got down to the business of playing hockey, he was as serious as the next guy."

Sillers couldn't help but tell the story about his boyhood chum returning to Saskatoon from Los Angeles at the end of a Western Hockey League season in the early 1960s. "Bobby had signed a decent contract with the WHL Blades and bought a brand new Pontiac Le Mans," Sillers says. "He couldn't wait to drive home to show it off to his friends. But somewhere outside of Idaho, somebody stole his bucket seats. When he arrived in Saskatoon, he was driving the car as he sat on a wooden crate. It kinda took the shine off his arrival."

On a more serious note, Sillers remembers Montreal Canadiens goaltending great Ken Dryden once being asked on national television which NHL forward's shot he most feared. "His answer," Sillers says, "was Mickey Redmond and Bobby Schmautz."

Saskatoon-born Schmautz was a problem for NHL goaltenders. He could unleash a deceptively hard shot, often catching them off guard.

GARY SMITH
A suitcase full of surprises

GARY (SUITCASE) SMITH TELEGRAPHED the message early in the 1974–75 NHL season that something very special was happening with the Vancouver Canucks.

It began with what Emile Francis described in later years as "one of the greatest goaltending performances of all time." Francis was head coach of the New York Rangers on the night of October 20, 1974, when Smith was flawless in a 1–0 Vancouver win at Madison Square Garden.

"We hadn't been shut out at home in 83 games," Francis told reporters after the game, "Then along comes Smitty and stones us despite being outshot 33–15. It didn't go over too well with our fans, who can get pretty ugly at the best of times."

For Smith and the upstart Canucks it marked the first time they had survived a lengthy road trip without a loss. After upsetting the Rangers, they returned to the Pacific Coliseum with wins against Toronto and St. Louis and a tie in Minnesota.

"I can remember Peter Stemkowski telling the New York media that they [the Rangers] could have played until two o'clock in the morning and still not scored on me," Smith says. "When I read that quote, I suggested if Stemkowski had seen me at 2 a.m. he would never have said such a thing."

Smith blanked the Chicago Blackhawks and Tony Esposito 1–0 three weeks later, prompting Canucks captain Chris Oddleifson to stand in the

Above: A curly-haired Smith was never at a loss for words with the media, home or away.

Left: Lanky Gary Smith displays his all-star, stand-up form during a successful 1974-75 season when the Canucks finished first in the Smythe Division.

Smith sprawls in spectacular fashion to foil a Boston Bruins scoring chance as Canucks defender Jocelyn Guevremont comes to his rescue.

centre of the dressing room and announce to his teammates: "We have a goaltender among us who will be heading to the All Star Game in a couple of months."

Oddleifson was right. Smith shared the all star assignment with Philadelphia's Bernie Parent and proceeded to lead the Canucks to a first-place, 86-point finish in the Smythe Division.

"I used to have fun with the out-of-town reporters and tell them the real secret to our success was the fact it was the first time we had a coach who could get along with our general manager," Smith jokes. "It would take them a little time to figure out that Phil Maloney held both jobs."

Maloney idolized Smith, and with good reason. The 6-foot-4 masked man led all NHL goaltenders by playing in 72 games, winning 32 of them and registering six shutouts.

But the romance didn't last.

"We were at a team Christmas party at Capilano Golf Club when Phil and I got into a bit of an argument," Smith recalls from his home in Solana Beach, California. "There had been trade rumours making the rounds and he [Maloney] said he'd swap me for Oakland's Gilles Meloche if he got the chance. I was going through some marital problems at the time and we'd won only 11 games prior to Christmas . . . it just wasn't a good time for my

He skated all the way from his own net to the Montreal Canadiens' blueline in an attempt to score before being decked.

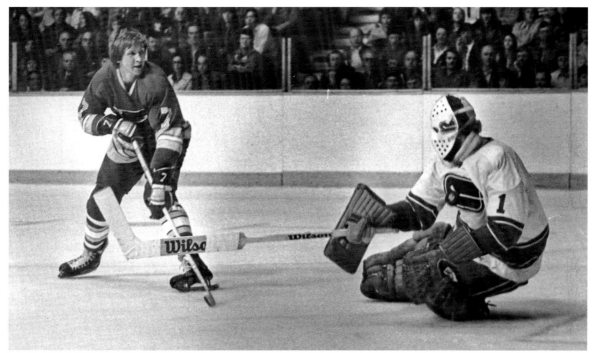

Smith thwarts St. Louis Blues centre Garry Unger in Johnny Bower-like fashion with an effective poke-check.

coach to be telling me he'd be willing to trade me. I said some things I shouldn't have and showed up at practice the next day wearing an Oakland Seals jacket over my sweater."

Not long after, the bloom came completely off the rose when, in front of a hometown crowd, Maloney pulled Smith out of a game against Pittsburgh after he had allowed five goals by the middle of the second period.

"Instead of going to the end of the bench like I was supposed to," Smith says, "I went straight to the dressing room, stripped off my gear, showered and went home. One of the newspaper guys wrote that I'd driven out of the parking lot still wearing my equipment and I didn't help matters by saying the next day how hard it was to be driving with skates on."

Smith was suspended without pay and despite the fact he suited up for 51 games that season, the

inevitable trade took place the following summer: Smith for Cesare Maniago of the Minnesota North Stars.

The man they called "Suitcase" travelled the NHL circuit for 14 years with six different teams. He once punted a puck in Maple Leaf Gardens that rang off the clock high above centre ice. He skated all the way from his own net to the Montreal Canadiens' blueline in an attempt to score before being decked by J.C. Tremblay. And he loved to tell make-believe stories to reporters.

"We had a lot of fun and I've got some great memories," Smith says.

"It's all different now, of course. I'm told the players go to their computers after games and analyze what they did that night, then send it to their agents for their corporate file. We analyzed our games, too, but it was over a pitcher of beer at the old Coach House in North Vancouver."

GRIFFITHS FAMILY
A legacy for the ages

Above: Frank Griffiths accepts one of many awards he received during his tenure as Chairman of the Board with the Vancouver Canucks.

Left: Canucks captain Stan Smyl (left) was presented with a portrait by North Vancouver artist Glen Green on the night of November 3, 1991, when Arthur and Frank Griffiths, Sr. (right) officiated in the retirement of Smyl's No. 12 jersey.

YOU CANNOT DISCUSS THE HISTORY of the Vancouver Canucks without discussing the Griffiths family and former owner Arthur Griffiths. Perhaps the link between owner and team was not quite the same as the New York Yankees and George Steinbrenner, or the Los Angeles Lakers and Jerry Buss, but it was close.

Starting with Frank Griffiths' purchase of the Canucks in 1974, the Vancouver family that built a broadcasting empire was identified with their hockey team for nearly a quarter century.

Arthur Griffiths went to work for his dad, Frank, straight out of college in the early 1980s. The son had giant dreams.

He dreamed of a Stanley Cup, yes. But he dreamed also of a glittering downtown arena, built

for the hockey team entirely with private funds. He dreamed of a National Basketball Association franchise, and a Canucks team rooted in its community and owned by British Columbians for British Columbians. And he dreamed, along with founders Brenda Eng and George Jarvis, of a beautiful and comforting place for ailing children and families.

Griffiths dreamed of so much that his story became a tale of Icarus, who soared joyously close to the sun before burning his wings and falling to earth.

By 1997, Arthur Griffiths had lost his share of everything after twice watching the Canucks make it to the Stanley Cup Final. But he built his arena, which saved the hockey team in Vancouver. And Canuck Place, the first dedicated children's hospice in North America, is the Griffiths family's greatest legacy.

"When I look at my life, sometimes it seems very surreal," says Arthur, still boyish despite flecks of grey hair. "I hardly know what was real and what wasn't anymore. I'll go to a game at GM Place and someone will say: 'What a great building you built.' I'll look up and say: 'Yeah, I guess so. We did build it.'"

Frank Griffiths, who died in 1994, less than two months before the Canucks' epic seven-game Stanley Cup Final loss to the New York Rangers,

In the early stages of construction of General Motors Place, the new home of the Canucks in downtown Vancouver began to take shape prior to its opening in 1995.

led a group that 20 years earlier had bought the franchise for $9 million from disgraced owner Thomas Scallen. The Minnesota businessman was convicted of securities fraud in 1973 after using funds raised in a public stock offering of the Canucks to repay a loan he took out to cover the original franchise fee.

The scandal clouded the Canucks' future.

"Coley Hall [a Canucks executive] basically came to my dad and said 'You need to get some people together so we can reclaim the team,' and he did," Arthur says. "He ended up owning more of the team than he wanted, but he was very proud to return it to local ownership. He was convinced it was important to have the team locally owned—at least locally controlled. He used to say, often, that this city and this country treated our family very

well, and [the purchase] was just to ensure the fans benefited from the team."

Arthur authored a new chapter in the family history when he announced in 1992 plans to build a downtown arena, after he concluded the franchise could not survive as a tenant at the Pacific Coliseum.

To help fill the new building, Griffiths secured a NBA expansion franchise that opened with General Motors Place in 1995.

The arena and basketball team cost more than $300 million, and Griffiths invited Seattle billionaire John McCaw into ownership.

With the loonie plummeting and threatening to cripple Canadian sports franchises, McCaw exercised options to increase his stake in the Canucks, Vancouver Grizzlies and GM Place.

Under a new street sign named in their honour by Vancouver Mayor Philip Owen, the Griffiths family was represented by sons Frank (left) and Arthur (right) and their proud mother Emily (centre).

"We got the privilege of writing the cheques and making decisions everyone criticized, but at the end of the day it still belonged to the fans."

"If Mr. McCaw hadn't continued to support the team financially, there would have been a significant risk of it not remaining in Vancouver," Canucks' Chief Operating Officer Victor de Bonis says. "It simply wasn't in his mindset to move the franchise or to sell it to someone who would move it.

"I was here working and living through that era when John McCaw's impact was a big and stabilizing part of the organization. He simply wanted to do the right thing to help keep the community asset in place."

McCaw eventually sold the Grizzlies in 2000 for US $165 million—NBA commissioner David Stern has said he regrets the league's lack of support for basketball in Vancouver—and completed the $250 million sale of the Canucks and GM Place to Vancouver's Aquilini family in 2006, once again restoring local ownership.

"What was I doing at my age running a hockey team?" Griffiths laughs now. "As much as this was hard to follow sometimes, we approached the ownership of the team as if we were kind of trustees. We got the privilege of writing the cheques and making decisions everyone criticized, but at the end of the day it still belonged to the fans."

In a way, it still does. Under the Aquilini family's stewardship, the Canucks are one of the most supported franchises in hockey. The team should remain in Vancouver in perpetuity. Arthur Griffiths would like that.

GARRY MONAHAN
Momentous goal in Montreal

THERE ARE TWO VERY DIFFERENT descriptive versions of one of the most significant goals in the history of the Vancouver Canucks.

It happened on a Tuesday night—April 15, 1975—at the Montreal Forum.

The Canucks were engaged in their first playoff series since joining the NHL in 1970. Or, as the late *Vancouver Sun* columnist Jim Kearney wrote: "A Vancouver hockey team is headed to the Stanley Cup playoffs for the first time since 1924 when the Vancouver Maroons lost to the Canadiens in the final that year."

The 1974–75 Canucks finished first in the Smythe Division of the Clarence Campbell Conference and drew Montreal as their quarter-final playoff opponents.

Over the course of five seasons, the talent-laden Habs had gone 27 games without losing to Vancouver, winning 24 and tying three.

After being pummelled 6–2 in the playoff opener at the Forum, the Canucks were listed as 50-to-1 long shots by oddsmakers in Las Vegas to register a single victory in the best-of-seven series.

But with the combination of splendid goaltending from Gary Smith and disciplined defensive play orchestrated by head coach Phil Maloney, the Canucks nailed their first-ever win over the Canadiens and their first-ever playoff victory, all on the same night.

Above: Monahan wrote NHL history by becoming the league's first-ever draft choice, selected by the Montreal Canadiens in 1963.

Left: A historic goal at the Montreal Forum in a 1975 playoff game put Garry Monahan in the national limelight.

Monahan wards off defender Ted Harris of the Philadelphia Flyers while driving the net against the notorious Broad Street Bullies.

Garry Monahan scored the winning goal at 13:46 of the third period, breaking an entertaining 1–1 tie before a *Hockey Night in Canada* television audience. Doug Risebrough had given the Habs the lead with a goal midway through the second period before Gerry O'Flaherty tied it four minutes later when he banged home a Bob Dailey rebound.

It stood tied until Monahan's momentous goal, described this way in the *Vancouver Sun*: "Monahan shot from 30 feet out and Ken Dryden made a glove save, only to have his own teammate—Leon Rochefort—collide with him and knock the puck from Dryden's glove into the Montreal net."

Which isn't even close to how Monahan remembers the most talked about goal of his 11-year NHL career.

"No, not all," Monahan says, tongue firmly entrenched in his cheek. "I recall it was an end-to-end rush that started behind Smith. I dipsy-doodled past Steve Shutt, Pete Mahovlich and Jacques Lemaire. Now it's a one-on-two against Carol Vadnais, or it could've been Larry Robinson, and Serge Savard. I got between them and went high with a blast to Dryden's glove side. It was a one-on-six, including Dryden."

All joking aside, Monahan refers to the goal as the high point of his career. "It tied the series and for a brief while we believed we could knock them off," he says. "When we returned to Vancouver for Games 3 and 4, our fans treated us like we were rock stars. The whole city was turned on. It was quite a thrill."

"I got between them and went high with a blast to Dryden's glove side. It was a one-on-six, including Dryden."

The Habs proceeded to win the next three games but the spunky Canucks did take them to overtime in Game 5 before being eliminated.

Monahan will always remain part of NHL history by being selected as the first-ever draft choice in the league when the Canadiens plucked him in the original amateur draft in 1963. A prolific scorer as a junior with the OHA Peterborough Petes, Monahan adopted the role of a hard-working defensive forward during NHL stops in Montreal, Detroit, Los Angeles, Toronto and Vancouver.

His NHL career ended as a Maple Leaf in 1978–79, but Monahan continued playing for three more seasons in Japan.

Upon his return to Canada, he finished an ongoing mission to acquire a teaching degree at the University of Toronto, when he was introduced to the broadcasting industry as a colour commentator with the Maple Leafs.

That led to an offer in Vancouver, where he worked as Jim Robson's analyst on CKNW Radio and with Dave Hodge on simulcast television coverage on BCTV.

"That run lasted about 10 years," Monahan says. "From there I became a stockbroker and eventually got into real estate with Royal LePage in West Vancouver."

Canucks loyalists have never forgotten Monahan's golden moment at the Montreal Forum in 1975. "Even 35 years later," Monahan says with a hint of shyness, "people stop me on the street or at a hockey game at GM Place and want to talk about it. I sure got a lot of mileage out of that goal."

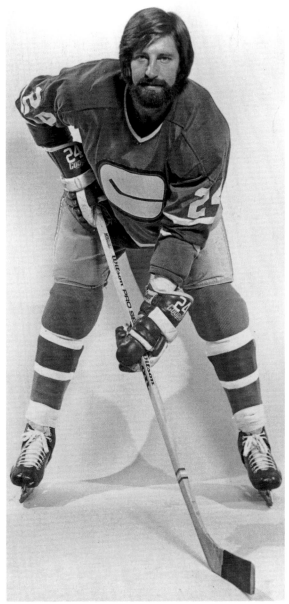

A television and radio career awaited Monahan at the conclusion of his NHL career.

DENNIS VERVERGAERT
Ten seconds of all-star glory

DENNIS VERVERGAERT WAS A RAMBUNCTIOUS, still maturing, 22-year-old winger with the Vancouver Canucks when he seemingly came out of nowhere to set an NHL All Star Game record that lasted for more than two decades.

All he did was score two goals in a 10-second span, and nearly a third on the same shift, as the Campbell Conference staged a furious rally in the final period that fell just short when the Wales Conference won 7–5.

It happened in the packed Spectrum at Philadelphia when Ververgaert, the only Canucks player selected for the mid-season game in 1976, got an opportunity to play on a forward line with New York Islanders star Bryan Trottier and another Isles player, Billy Harris. It was a performance that signalled Ververgaert's arrival as a genuine goal scorer, a player that opposing teams must respect.

To set the stage, the 1975–76 season was Ververgaert's third in the NHL, after playing junior with the London Knights. He was drafted third overall by the Canucks in 1973 and produced 26- and 19-goal seasons his first two years in Vancouver.

Ververgaert's third pro season proved to be his best, highlighted by an incredible performance in Philadelphia before 16,436 fans and most of the game's best players.

"It was kind of funny because the coach was Fred Shero [of the Philadelphia Flyers] and he

Above: Ververgaert studied the game intently during his early pro years and had a deft touch around the net when scoring chances materialized.

Left: From Grimsby, Ontario, to the bright lights of the NHL, Ververgaert enjoyed his playing days in Vancouver, where he remained to establish himself in the business community.

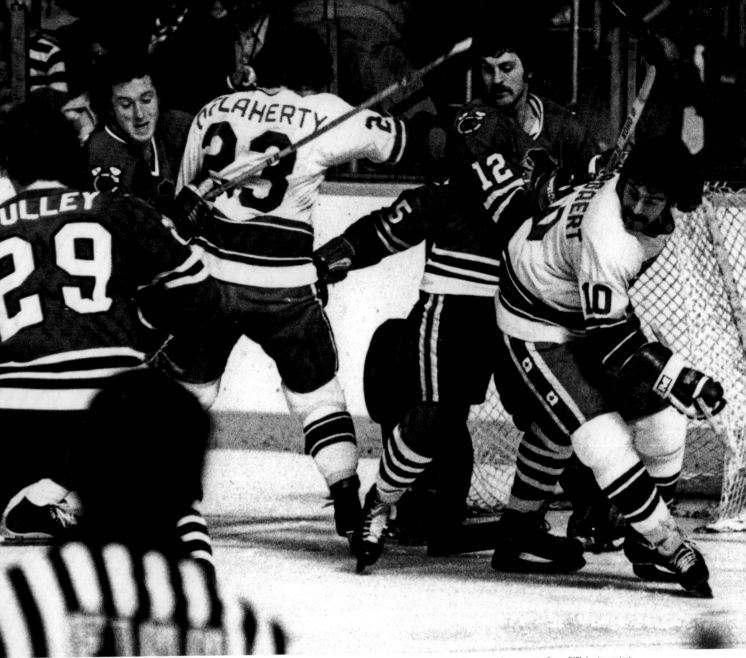

Ververgaert's No. 10 uniform could often be found in goalmouth action as he pressed for scoring chances like this one with teammate Gerry O'Flaherty against Chicago, while being checked by Ivan Boldirev and Ted Bulley of the Blackhawks.

told me before the game I was going to have to play on the off-wing," recalls Ververgaert. "It was the first time for me because I had always played right wing. That was a scary thing for me right off the bat. The game got kind of one-sided and the Wales had a 7–1 lead after two periods. Then we started to get some scoring chances."

Ververgaert didn't waste his opportunities against Wales netminder Wayne Thomas from the Toronto Maple Leafs. Thomas had replaced starter Ken Dryden of the Montreal Canadiens at the midway point of the game.

"Trottier made three plays to me that were almost identical, all from the one corner," Ververgaert says. "Being on the off-wing, I had a lot more net to shoot at than normally.

"We got the one goal [at 4:33 of the third] and from the faceoff he shot the puck into their zone again. He was pretty fast and beat everybody to the puck in the corner, got the puck to me and boom, it was in again [at 4:43], a replay of the first one. Right after that, I hit the post.

"I couldn't believe it. With all the name players in the game, like Peter Mahovlich and Guy Lafleur from Montreal, it kind of surprised me when the goals happened. Shero kept putting us out every second shift, it seemed, and we managed to make it a closer game."

Ververgaert's third season with the Canucks turned out to be his most productive and certainly most memorable.

Ververgaert would go on to lead the Canucks in scoring that season with 37 goals and 71 points, totals he would never surpass during an NHL career that lasted eight seasons and ended prematurely because of shoulder injuries.

He would play in another NHL All Star Game in 1979 in Buffalo at Memorial Auditorium, but was unable to score when the Wales won again, this time 3–2 on an overtime goal by Gilbert Perreault of the Buffalo Sabres.

Looking back, Ververgaert considered himself fortunate to have played in two NHL All Star Games at such a young age. He was still an emerging player and surrounded by his peers.

"It was such a great honour to be there and associated with guys like Lafleur," Ververgaert says. "I knew I didn't have that kind of talent. To be in the same [dressing] room almost left me in awe. It was kind of overwhelming.

"After the first game, I remember the Vancouver owners [the Griffiths family] inviting me to their hotel room to attend a private party. A lot of people circled around me there and made me feel special. To have that kind of attention was different because usually I shied away from that kind of stuff. Looking back, it was kind of neat."

Ververgaert usually shied away from publicity, although he enjoyed the attention when it came from Canucks ownership.

Looking back, Ververgaert considered himself fortunate to have played in two NHL All Star Games at such a young age.

Ververgaert got to meet several of the Flyers during his first All Star Game when the Campbell Conference team included Philadelphia players Bill Barber, Andre Dupont, Reggie Leach, Wayne Stephenson and Jim Watson. Three years later, Ververgaert would be traded to Philadelphia.

"I think Philly got interested in me because of that NHL All Star Game," says Ververgaert. "I really liked Shero, but by the time I got to Philly, he had gone to New York."

A proud Ververgaert accepts the Cyrus H. McLean Trophy as the team's leading scorer in 1975-76 from Hockey Hall of Fame member Walter (Babe) Pratt while PA announcer Tom Peacock watches the presentation.

Ververgaert always appreciated the treatment he was given by Canucks staff, and also by Pacific Coliseum manager Mario Caravetta, who in 1978 arranged for Ververgaert to be married in the Dogwood Room on the grounds of Pacific National Exhibition near the Coliseum.

"I got married in March during the hockey season and that night we were also listening for the Chicago result because it mattered to us in the standings," Ververgaert remembers. "It turned out to be a great evening all the way around."

As for that NHL All Star Game record, it lasted 21 years, until Owen Nolan of the San Jose Sharks scored twice in eight seconds for the West team in the 1997 game at San Jose.

"I really enjoyed the Vancouver area and made it my home after I retired," said Ververgaert. "I remember, before the draft, my advisors assured me I'd be selected by the Leafs. Vancouver picked just ahead of Toronto, though, so the Leafs ended up with Lanny McDonald. In the end, it all worked out for the best."

BABE PRATT
A beloved legend

Florence Pratt sensed something wasn't quite right as she and her husband of 51 years drove to the Pacific Coliseum on the night of December 16, 1988, for the Canucks game against the Calgary Flames.

Her beloved and legendary Babe hadn't been himself all day.

Sure enough, his ritual on a Canucks game night changed. He spent more time than usual with the arena attendants who hung out in the boiler room, and Florence had to tug at his sleeve as he later stood in an almost frozen state behind the glass at the south end of the rink.

Normally he would walk Florence to her seat in the stands and leave her to settle in on her own while he hustled off to the press box. "But on this night he reached out and squeezed Mom's hand, told her to enjoy the game and kissed her on the cheek," son Tracy recalls. "That was totally out of character for him."

Tracy, who had played his entire career as "Babe Pratt's son," was also at the game with his youngest daughter, Shannon. "It was six or seven minutes into the second period when they announced over the public address system that I was to report immediately to the press box," Tracy says. "I turned to Shannon and said: 'Stay right here; don't move. Something's wrong with Grandpa.'"

Above: The warm, friendly smile of Walter (Babe) Pratt was his lovable trademark.

Left: The Babe shared his hockey knowledge with all ages. He talked, they listened.

Babe the goodwill ambassador helps a young fan drop a ceremonial puck at Pacific Coliseum for captains Stan Smyl of the Canucks and Dale Hawerchuk of the Winnipeg Jets.

The first person Tracy ran into at the top of the media area stairs was television sportscaster John McKeachie. He remembers McKeachie saying: "You don't want to go in there."

Walter (Babe) Pratt, 72, had suffered a massive heart attack and lay on the floor of the press box lounge with Canucks doctor Dave Harris and six paramedics standing over him. Canucks team owner Arthur Griffiths and general manager Pat Quinn were there, too.

Dr. Harris told Tracy to contact his mom, who'd already made her way from the far side of the Coliseum to the press box. Florence joined Babe in the ambulance; Tracy drove behind, with young Shannon in the passenger seat.

Babe drew his final breath en route to Vancouver General Hospital with Florence gently rubbing his hand.

"He always said he wanted to die with his hockey boots on," says Tracy, a 10-year NHL defenceman who played three seasons in Vancouver. "Dad loved the Canucks; he loved the players, the fans and the media. And they loved him back."

A proud native of Stony Mountain, Manitoba, Babe signed with the New York Rangers as a tough, hard-hitting defenceman at the age of 18. He was a Stanley Cup champion with the Rangers in 1939–40 and the Toronto Maple Leafs in 1944–45, the year he won the Hart Trophy as the NHL's most valuable player.

"Dad loved the Canucks; he loved the players, the fans and the media. And they loved him back."

Three generations of Pratts: When Tracy was 15 years old he went to a WHL Canucks camp. His support crew included his dad Babe (right) and Charlie Pratt, Tracy's grandpa.

Babe finished his career as a player-coach in the old Pacific Coast Hockey League with the New Westminster Royals and Tacoma Rockets in the early 1950s.

He kept his hand—and face—in the game by appearing with host Brad Keene on a weekly NHL black-and-white television show based in Bellingham, Washington, sponsored by El Producto Cigars.

Babe's real job was inspecting and buying lumber for MacDonald Cedar in Fort Langley. When the expansion Canucks went looking for a King Clancy-type goodwill ambassador in the summer of 1970, Pratt was hired on the basis of one phone call.

Babe was the "face" of the Canucks organiztion during its infant years. He spread his storytelling wit and never-ending charm among hockey fans throughout British Columbia and across the country as colour commentator with CBC's *Hockey Night in Canada*.

A member of the NHL Hockey Hall of Fame, the Manitoba Sports Hall of Fame and the Kenora Hall of Fame, Babe has never been similarly recognized in B.C., despite his 18 years of dedication to the Vancouver Canucks.

"When they ask," says Tracy, "I'll tell them they're too late."

HAROLD SNEPSTS
"Harr-old, Harr-old" a familiar chant

HAROLD SNEPSTS HAD A REWARDING 12-year run with the Vancouver Canucks, when the helmetless, mustachioed defenceman was arguably the team's most popular player for many of those NHL seasons.

Cheers would come cascading down from the upper bowl when he was on the ice at the Pacific Coliseum. "Harr-old, Harr-old" was the preferred chant as fans constantly showed their appreciation for a player who referred to himself as merely a "hard-working, blue-collar, lunch-pail player."

The Edmonton-born Snepsts was such a fan favourite that later, long after his playing career was over, he would be named by Global TV as one of the seven greatest Canucks of all time.

Snepsts was a stay-at-home defender who liked to block shots for his goaltender and could get into a rousing fight when he thought teammates were being abused by the opposition. He soon became a cult hero when he joined the team during his first pro season in 1974–75, after being drafted in the third round by Vancouver from the Edmonton Oil Kings.

By the 1976–77 season, he was a stalwart on the Vancouver defence. He recalls going to a football game in Seattle on a day off and teammates discussing who should represent the Canucks in the 1977 NHL All Star Game, the first to be staged in Vancouver.

Above: With his Clint Eastwood-like good looks, a young Snepsts became an instant fan favourite with his dashing play at the Pacific Coliseum.

Left: An always aware Harold Snepsts was adept at moving the puck effectively from the defensive zone.

Never, not even for a fleeting moment, did Snepsts expect that the player Vancouver fans often called "Dirty Harry" would be their representative in the 30th NHL All Star Game.

"By the time I got there, I was so nervous I could hardly tie my skates," he remembers. "It must have taken five or six attempts before I got them tied.

"I was on the Campbell Conference team coached by Fred Shero. There were a lot of Philadelphia Flyers on the team and they were a pretty tight group. I remember during the game,

"We were just a bunch of guys that worked hard for each other."

when Phil Esposito got hit by Borje Salming, the Flyer guys were ready to go after Salming."

Snepsts's defensive partner in the NHL All Star Game was Jim Watson of the Flyers. The other Campbell defencemen were Tom Bladon and Joe Watson from Philadelphia, Phil Russell of the Chicago Blackhawks and Denis Potvin of the New York Islanders. Snepsts was in elite company and so proud to represent his team.

The game was a see-saw affair and the sellout Coliseum crowd of 15,607 followed every shift for Snepsts with its usual enthusiasm.

Eric Vail of the Atlanta Flames gave the Campbell team a lead in the first period before the Wales squad equalized on a goal by Lanny McDonald of the Toronto Maple Leafs. Philadelphia's Rick MacLeish put the Campbells ahead again in the second period, but the Wales team countered on another goal by McDonald.

In the third period, with the score tied 2–2, Rick Martin of the Buffalo Sabres took over the spotlight. He scored on goalie Glenn (Chico) Resch of the New York Islanders for a 3–2 Wales lead at the four-minute mark.

Esposito, representing the New York Rangers, tied the game for a third time at 12:23, beating Buffalo Sabres netminder Gerry Desjardins.

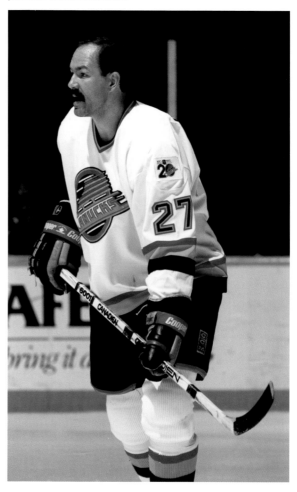

Big No.27 demanded the respect of opposing players with his willingness to protect his Vancouver teammates.

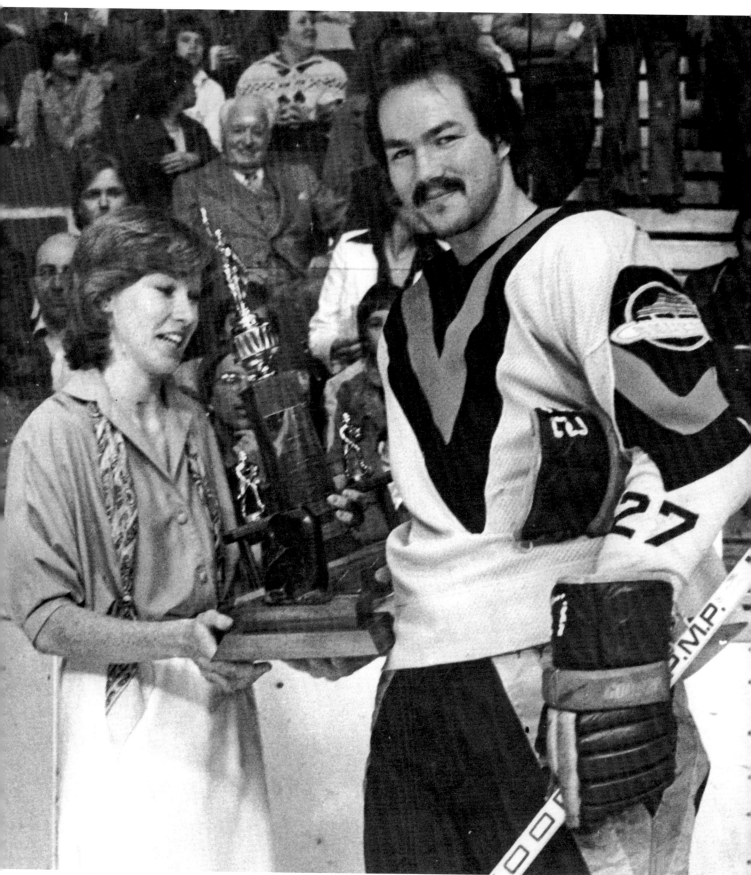

Canucks fans made their feelings known towards the player they affectionately called "Dirty Harry."

Snepsts provided a comfort zone for Canucks goaltenders like Richard Brodeur.

A four-time winner of the Babe Pratt trophy, Snepsts became a close friend of Pratt.

That set the stage for Martin to become the game's most valuable player when he scored the game-winner and his second marker of the night at 18:04, assisted by Marcel Dionne of the Los Angeles Kings and Guy Lafleur of the Montreal Canadiens.

Still, in the minds of most fans that memorable night, they were enthused that their local favourite, a player who once fought rival Doug Risebrough under the stands during a game and was suspended five games, had represented his team with aplomb.

"I came to Vancouver as a young player and made the city my new home," Snepsts says. "People accepted me for what I was. My only disappointment was we couldn't bring home the Stanley Cup for them. I would have given everything up, including that NHL All Star Game, for a Cup for Vancouver."

Snepsts and the Canucks made it to the Stanley Cup Final a few years later with convincing series wins over Calgary, Los Angeles and Chicago before falling in four games to the New York Islanders.

"That was quite a run in '82, because our confidence grew with every series," says Snepsts. "We were a very close team with no superstars. We were just a bunch of guys that worked hard for each other.

"Richard Brodeur was great in goal and we won a lot of games in overtime. The injuries hurt, especially on defence, but it gave some of the younger guys a chance. Neil Belland was terrific in the playoffs, blocking shots and keeping his composure. We had the time of our lives."

Snepsts was a defensive defenceman, of course, but he did manage to score 38 NHL goals, including one on a penalty shot February 2, 1980, against Minnesota North Stars goaltender Gilles Meloche.

"We were in Minny and we were killing a penalty, two men short, playing the triangle," Snepsts recalls. "Don Lever blocked a shot and I charged up the ice and got into the clear and got tripped. I fell into the net and Meloche was on top of me. Lever told me to stay down, or something like that.

"Harry Neale was the coach and had me take the penalty shot. I was just trying to hit the net, that's all. Believe it or not, we won 5–4."

Harold Snepsts was inducted into the B.C. Hockey Hall of Fame in 2004.

He's also a member of the B.C. Sports Hall of Fame (2006) and was hired as a scout by the Canucks in 2009.

STAN SMYL

"Steamer" first to the rafters

IF PUNCH MCLEAN HAD HAD HIS WAY, Stan Smyl would have been a Red Wing.

How so? McLean had coached the stocky winger in four Memorial Cup tournaments for the New Westminster Bruins, the latter two being series champions. And no player had been more instrumental in the junior team's success than Stanley Phillip Smyl of St. Paul, Alberta.

During the 1978 NHL amateur draft, McLean, wearing his second hat as a scout with Detroit, recommended to Wings general manager Ted Lindsay that they take Smyl with their third pick. But the Wings also had their eyes on another WHL winger, Glenn Hicks from Flin Flon, Manitoba.

"Who's the better skater?" Lindsay asked McLean.

"I gotta say Hicks," replied Punch. "But Smyl's got way better leadership qualities."

With that, Detroit chose Hicks, and Smyl lasted another 12 selections before it was Vancouver's turn to draft. New West GM Bill Shinske yelled over to Canucks GM Jake Milford that Smyl was still available. Milford had secured the players he wanted in the first two rounds—high-scoring Bill Derlago of Brandon and hard-nosed Curt Fraser from Victoria—so maybe he would take a flyer on the kid nicknamed "Steamer."

Still, Milford was skeptical. The trend at the time dictated drafting big, strong skaters and Smyl

Above: It didn't take long for the serious Smyl to become a fan favourite at the Pacific Coliseum as he excited the crowd with his determination to succeed, regardless of the situation.

Left: Smyl credits his Prairie upbringing for the leadership qualities he displayed for more than a decade with the Canucks. The gritty right winger wore the captaincy proudly.

Smyl always drove the net hard and stopped near the crease, making life miserable for the likes of New York Islanders goaltender Billy Smith.

was listed at 5-foot-8 and deemed a slow skater by most NHL scouts. But after much thought, the Canucks opted for Smyl.

It turned out that the Canucks drafted a special player who would endear himself to Vancouver fans for more than a decade with the hustle, grit and determination that made him a clear leader.

"As a kid in minor hockey, you have dreams about someday playing in the NHL," Smyl says. "Things just seemed to come naturally to me much of the time. A lot of it, especially the leadership, has to do with your upbringing. I always watched and listened to my parents (Pauline and Bernard) and my minor hockey coaches. You see what it takes to win, the little things that help along the way.

"The biggest reason I made it to the National Hockey League, I believe, was my work ethic. I was content with doing that, night after night. And I learned in junior what it meant to assist your teammates when help was needed."

McLean guided Smyl's steady growth during four years with New Westminster when the Bruins were the most feared western team in junior hockey, with their robust style, led by the omnipresent Smyl.

"The desire to succeed was always there with Stan because he had had such great role models at home," McLean says. "His leadership was unquestioned and he later managed to play with the same heart and desire as a professional."

Smyl's personality was contagious, and it seeped through enough of his teammates to make the Canucks a miserable team to play against.

Smyl led the Canucks in goals, assists, points and penalty minutes during the 1979-80 season, a rare accomplishment in the NHL.

When the Canucks opened their 1978 training camp in Courtenay, B.C., it didn't take long for Smyl to make an impact. During an early scrimmage, Smyl ran veteran defenceman Harold Snepsts (6-foot-3, 215 pounds) against the end boards so hard that the collision dislodged a whole section of the Plexiglas and play had to be suspended while repairs were made. Eyebrows were raised all around. What a hit by a raw rookie on a seasoned veteran! But this was just the first sign of a ferocious checking style that would characterize Smyl's entire NHL career. He may have been only 185 pounds, but he sure played a lot bigger than that, earning the nickname "Steamer" for his tenacious efforts.

In the season opener, new Canucks head coach Harry Neale iced a line that consisted of all rookies. Swedish centre Thomas Gradin had Curt Fraser on his left side and Smyl on his right. Neale looked like a genius as Gradin scored two goals and an assist, Fraser a goal and an assist, and Smyl chipped in with one assist as Vancouver hammered visiting Colorado, 8–2. Needless to say, the line remained intact all season.

Smyl would go on to record a respectable 14 goals, 24 assists and 38 points in his freshman year, despite missing 18 games through injury.

But it was during the following season that he made a name for himself around the NHL. That's when he blossomed into a bona fide NHL star, leading the Canucks in goals (31), assists (47), points (78) and penalty minutes (204), a feat not equalled in the NHL until Joe Thornton led in all four categories with Boston in 1999–2000.

Over the next eight seasons, Smyl would deliver on a consistent basis, never scoring fewer than 20 goals and three times topping 30. He was

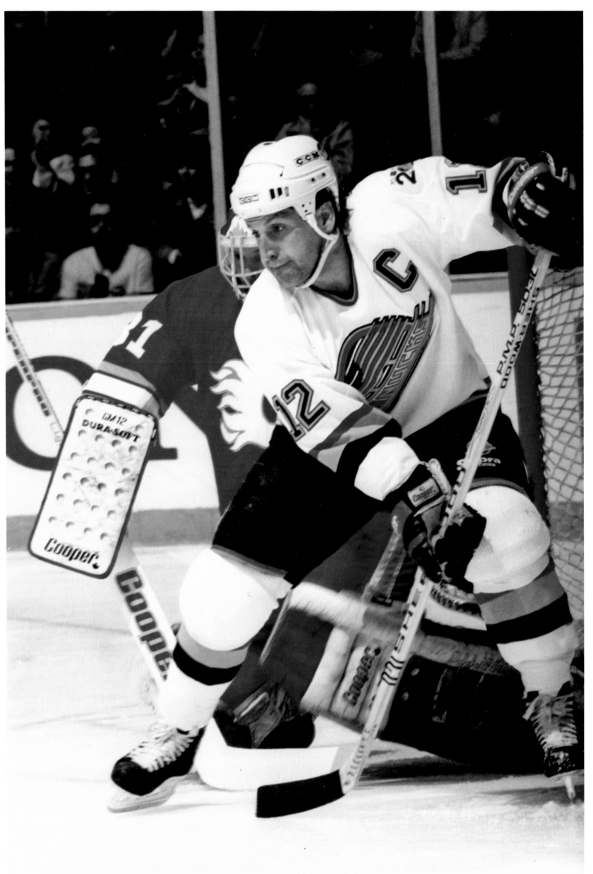

Smyl became "Mr. Consistent" in the scoring department by going eight consecutive seasons with 20 or more goals, and three times topping the 30-goal plateau.

Smyl played some of his best games against the top teams as he got the job done against premiere players, including the Islanders.

also consistent in his delivery of bone-jarring body checks and stayed true to his hard-nosed style of play, which resulted in nine 100-plus penalty-minute seasons.

Smyl's personality was contagious, too, and it seeped through enough of his teammates to make the Canucks a miserable team to play against. This was never truer than in the spring of 1982 when Smyl & Co. swashbuckled their way to the Stanley Cup Final. Along the way, they dispatched Calgary, Los Angeles and Chicago through a relentless work ethic and a wolf-pack attitude. And while they didn't win Lord Stanley's coveted mug, Smyl and the Canucks gained league-wide respect.

Smyl's leadership, both on and off the ice, had become immense and, prior to the 1982–83 season, the "C" was sewn onto his No. 12 sweater.

He played the captain's role with pride and aplomb for the next eight seasons. Smyl would never be described as flashy, but he never took a night off, patrolling his wing with total dedication. With honesty and integrity, he simply got the job done.

At the conclusion of the 1990–91 campaign, the crashing and banging of 13 NHL seasons had taken its toll on the 33-year-old warrior and Smyl decided to call it a career.

On November 3, 1991, Vancouver bestowed the team's highest honour upon the man often called the heart and soul of the Canucks. Surrounded by his family, friends, and team owners, and in front of a full house, they hoisted a huge No. 12 banner to the rafters of the Pacific Coliseum.

But that's not the end of the story. Smyl's playing legacy morphed into a splendid off-ice career with the Canucks. Over the years since his retirement as a player, he has filled many roles, including assistant coach, head coach of the Canucks' farm team, director of player personnel, director of collegiate scouting, and senior advisor to the general manager.

GLEN HANLON
The night "The Franchise" shocked Montreal

GLEN HANLON WAS A RED-HEADED goaltending prodigy, drafted by Vancouver in 1977 when the Canucks already had veterans Cesare Maniago and Curt Ridley under contract. It didn't take long for Hanlon, the pride of Brandon, Manitoba, to earn the nickname "The Franchise."

When it came time for Vancouver's pick in the third round, Canucks general manager Jake Milford didn't hesitate in taking Hanlon with the 40th selection from the Brandon Wheat Kings. After all, Milford was partial to Manitobans because he also hailed from that area.

There were 21 goaltenders selected in the 1977 NHL draft and it's fair to claim that Hanlon was at least the equal of noted NHL goalies Pete Peeters and Greg Millen, both drafted later than Hanlon.

Hanlon would go on to play in 477 NHL games, including 133 with the Canucks. Hanlon recorded his first NHL shutout on November 1, 1978, a 1–0 Vancouver decision in Chicago over the Blackhawks. Then, on November 18, 1979, Hanlon became the first Canucks goaltender to win a regular-season game against the mighty Montreal Canadiens, a 5–2 decision at the Pacific Coliseum, with Ron Sedlbauer putting an insurance marker into an empty net, to the delight of giddy fans. The Canucks had proven, thanks to the brilliance of Hanlon, that they belonged in the same rink as the storied Habs.

Above: A graduate of the junior Brandon Wheat Kings, Hanlon had quick hands and acrobatic style.

Left: Glen Hanlon's southpaw stance was a roadblock for the Habs on a history-making night at the Pacific Coliseum.

"Going into that game, both Gary Bromley and I were injured," recalls Hanlon. "Before the game, we both were unsure who could play. We both went out for warmup and I ended up playing.

"It was a great win. I can still remember after the game how excited the fans were about winning a regular-season game against the Canadiens. The enthusiasm was almost overwhelming. Afterwards, Stan Smyl and I just looked at each other in the dressing room. We were thinking, 'There's no better place in the world right now.'

"I remember making a couple of glove saves on [Guy] Lafleur. In those days, the highlight save was always a big glove save. It's just the way we played back then. I don't remember all the specifics, just the overall feeling of how great this really was, and what could be."

Hanlon didn't like coming off the ice when he was a skater, so he moved permanently to goal from defence.

It wasn't long before fans and media were calling Hanlon "The Franchise." He had helped shut down a team that had so many future Hall of Fame players. Lafleur, Steve Shutt and Jacques Lemaire come to mind, along with Larry Robinson. It was an all star lineup, for sure.

"Montreal didn't spend much time in their own end," Hanlon says. "But on that night, we played so well.

"We had great people, too, in those years. I remember Don Lever being a terrific captain, also a tremendous person. Stan Smyl, I have nothing but respect for what he's done. Dennis Ververgaert and Ron Sedlbauer. They all treated me very well. I also remember Claire Alexander, who everyone called 'The Milkman.' He was a great help to me when I was a young pro playing in Tulsa. He was there to support me at all times."

Hanlon's name can be linked to another event in 1979 that stands out in hockey history. He was in goal for the Canucks when Wayne Gretzky scored his first NHL goal for the Edmonton Oilers on October 14.

"I guess for a goaltender, when your claim to fame is letting in a goal, that is not really something to be famous for," jokes Hanlon. "I kind of laugh when people say I let Gretzky score. We all

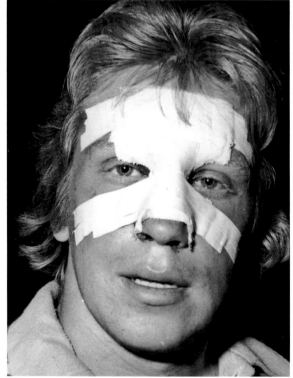

The "bandage look" was not the type of mask that goaltender Hanlon preferred to wear.

knew at the time that he was going to become a great player, but nobody could ever forecast how great he was going to be.

"It was a goal where he kind of came from behind the net to score. I couldn't recall it until I started to see highlights when he was going for Gordie Howe's record. I had to remind myself to

Canucks forward Pit Martin gives the falling Hanlon a helping hand in making a clearance.

recall the goal. It was kind of typical for Gretzky, where he hung onto the puck long enough to make you look silly."

Hanlon's quick glove hand and acrobatic style allowed him to play long enough to establish his credibility. He would also play for the New York Rangers and the Detroit Red Wings before his playing career ended with the 1990–91 season.

He had started playing goal as a youth in Brandon because his older brother, Ward, needed someone to take shots at in the back yard. Hanlon also didn't like coming off the ice when he was a skater, so he moved permanently to goal from defence.

He would later win 167 NHL games in the regular season and another 11 in the playoffs. His

Molson (B.C.) president Hal Moran with Molson Cup winner Hanlon, who won the award in back-to-back seasons for receiving the most game-star selections during the regular season.

goals-against average wasn't always pretty, but his effort was never questioned. Opposing teams always had great respect for Hanlon, even in junior, when the Brandon Wheat Kings often duelled with the tough New Westminster Bruins coached by Ernie (Punch) McLean.

"We had some terrific players in Brandon, playing for coach Dunc McCallum," recalls Hanlon. "Brad McCrimmon was a first-round pick. So was Laurie Boschman. Bill Derlago, Brian Propp and Ray Allison went on to be first-rounders. In all, we had five first-rounders, two thirds and Dave Semenko. New West had good players, too, a lot more physical than us. They nullified a lot of the effectiveness of our young players."

Bruins coach McLean was so impressed by Hanlon that he picked up the Brandon netminder as injury insurance in the playoffs one year. Hanlon got into four games in the 1976 Memorial Cup and posted a 2–1 record.

Over the years, Hanlon studied the game so well that he was in a position to become a goaltending coach, then a head coach in the NHL, and also an international coach in the World Championships.

Hanlon worked with netminder Kirk McLean during Vancouver's run to a second Stanley Cup Final in 1994. After four years as a Canucks assistant, Hanlon moved to the American Hockey League to become head coach of the Portland Pirates. Three years later he was back in the NHL, first as an assistant, then as head coach of the Washington Capitals.

In Washington, Hanlon got to work with Alexander Ovechkin, the Russian scoring machine with so much charisma and love for the game.

"It's almost like having a day off because you never have to motivate him," says Hanlon. "I always felt his biggest attribute was Ovie's ability to make everyone around him love hockey. He does everything with enthusiasm and a smile on his face."

Hanlon can relate. He has the same endearing qualities.

HARRY NEALE
Wild ride to first Stanley Cup Final

THE TRIO OF JAKE MILFORD, HARRY NEALE and Roger Neilson established a freshly minted respect for the Vancouver franchise in the spring of 1982, orchestrating the Canucks' first appearance in the Stanley Cup Final.

Jake Milford was the architect as general manager, with Harry Neale the head coach of record, and Roger Neilson the respected assistant coach who substituted after Neale was suspended by the NHL near the end of the 1981–82 regular season.

They combined to produce a team that went 13–2 in the first three rounds of the playoffs, with series wins over Calgary, Los Angeles and Chicago, before falling to the New York Islanders in straight games in the Final.

"It was a great ride, something we'll always remember, a Cinderella story," recalls Neale. "Our credibility as a franchise was on the rise."

Milford was a cagey hockey man who arrived in Vancouver in 1977 and hired Neale the following year because Milford wanted a fresh approach. The Canucks got just that, as Neale was an engaging sort who was never lost for words.

Neale brought in the quirky Neilson, known in hockey circles as "Captain Video", and the Canucks had formed the staff for playoff success.

Neale to this day has no idea why Milford selected him to coach the Canucks, other than he had taken the Hartford-based New England Whalers to the WHA finals before losing to the Winnipeg Jets.

"I didn't know Jake and had no idea how he heard of me," Neale says. "He just called one day and wanted to talk. In those days, most of the coaches in the WHA would have liked to coach in the NHL.

Above: Fun-loving coach Neale was rarely at a loss for words.

Left: Scoreboard gazing wasn't always a pretty picture for Harry Neale and his staff.

Neale shares a moment with hockey's "godfather," Sam Pollock.

"WHA teams were failing financially, so when I got a chance to go to the NHL, I took it. Jake was a fine man and easy to work for. He gave me his ideas, but certainly there was no coaching. He was a manager. It was a healthy situation."

Neale was from Sarnia, Ontario, and had met Neilson when they played baseball as teenagers in the Toronto area. They also played Junior B hockey against each other, Neilson for Woodbridge and Neale for Weston. Later, Neale would instruct at Neilson's summer hockey schools and clinics.

"I followed his career closely," says Neale. "When he became available after working for Buffalo, it seemed natural to have him coach with us in Vancouver. His dedication was second to none. I always felt he was the hardest-working coach I'd ever been associated with."

During the 1981–82 season, when Thomas Gradin became the first Vancouver player to have

an 80-point season and Stan Smyl scored 34 goals in his sophomore NHL campaign, the Canucks had a 26–33–16 record after 75 games with Neale behind the bench.

Vancouver went east late in the schedule and won 4–2 in Montreal on March 18, ending the Canadiens' string of 29 unbeaten games at home. Two nights later, in Quebec City, the Canucks were tied 3–3 with the Nordiques in the third period when all hell broke loose.

Canucks winger Tiger Williams ran Peter Stastny hard into the boards and Wilf Paiement of the Nordiques came to the rescue of his teammate. Then, along the boards, a fan reached around the glass and took a poke at Williams, one of the most penalized NHL players.

That's when Neale got involved with the fan. The ensuing donnybrook involving players and the crowd was frowned upon by league executives

A pensive Neale considers his next move from behind the Canucks bench.

and turned a 30–33–17 season for 77 points into a run to the sacred Stanley Cup Final.

Milford had planned to retire after the 1981–82 season and have Neale become general manager. The idea was to have Neilson become the next head coach the following season.

"But I got suspended and Roger had the team going better than I had at the time of the suspension, so I just had Roger continue on during the playoffs for the good of the team," says Neale. "He got his head coaching job in April and May, rather than later.

"Those playoffs were a thrilling experience and I was caught up in it like a lot of the fans. I kind of wished I was still coaching, but I knew where I was going to be the next year and Roger had the team playing better than they ever had before.

"We were on a roll going into the Final and played pretty well those first two games against the Islanders. We quickly found out that trying to win four of the next five was impossible. They just shut us down at home. But what a great ride it was for the longest time.

In typical, quick-witted fashion, Neale concludes: "Our wins were harder to find than Jimmy Hoffa."

Jake Milford was the architect as general manager, with Harry Neale the head coach of record, and Roger Neilson the respected assistant coach.

and Neale was handed a 10-game suspension which carried over into the playoffs.

Neilson became head coach, eventually for the balance of the season. The Canucks finished the regular season 4–0–1 under Neilson and carried the momentum into the playoffs.

Neale's indiscretion turned into a defining moment for the Canucks, who rallied behind Neilson

SEARCH FOR TALENT
Canucks ventured overseas in difficult political times

ONE OF THE DEFINING MOMENTS for Vancouver management came when the Canucks elected to expand their horizons in the global search for players, a strategy that saw them reach into Europe and behind the Iron Curtain.

The pioneer in this regard was Canucks general manager Jake Milford, who recognized in the late 1970s the need to expand scouting efforts to faraway arenas in Sweden, Finland, Czechoslovakia and the Soviet Union.

The importing of players would contribute to Vancouver becoming a Stanley Cup contender.

The talent hunt would net the Canucks skilled players from Thomas Gradin of Sweden to Ivan Hlinka and Jiri Bubla of Czechoslovakia, plus several Soviets, including Igor Larionov and Pavel Bure. The importation would lead to Vancouver teams being more about skill than brawn.

"In the late 1970s the mentality of a lot of teams was that you couldn't win with European players," recalls Harry Neale, Vancouver's head coach, 1978–82. "We learned with Thomas Gradin and Lars Lindgren they could play and contribute at the NHL level."

Milford was a crafty sort and arranged for his scouting staff to search far and wide for players that might fit Vancouver's needs. NHL scouts were hardly welcome in foreign arenas, however, as hockey people in those countries recognized the pitfalls of

Above: Proudly showing his Czechoslovakian heritage, Jiri Bubla became part of an intriguing international invasion for the Canucks.

Left: Thomas Gradin, the fearless, hard-working Swede signed with the Canucks in 1981.

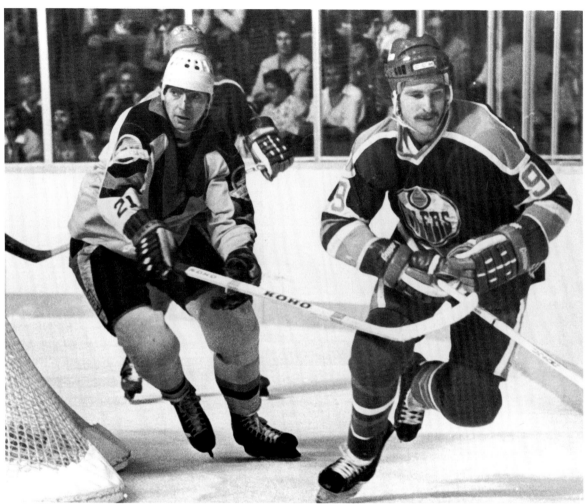

Czech-born centre Ivan Hlinka (21) matches strides with Edmonton Oiler winger Glenn Anderson.

too many players leaving for the best league in the world, even though the financial implications—payment for departing players—was appealing.

One of the first moves to upgrade Vancouver's talent base was to trade with Chicago for the rights to Gradin, a Swedish player the Canucks had scouted several times, including at the World Junior Championship.

"Jake really cranked things up when it came to bringing in foreign players," says Mike Penny, a Vancouver-based pro scout for 20 years. "We went to Europe and the Eastern Bloc countries on a regular basis. I remember going to a couple World Juniors over there and there would be only seven or eight scouts, mostly from European teams.

"We got Gradin because Jake had a guy working for him in Göteborg that really liked Thomas. I remember our guy over there saying that

[Chicago general manager Bob] Pulford didn't even talk with Gradin about coming to the NHL. We gave up only a second-round pick for the rights to Gradin, signed him right away. What a steal he turned out to be."

Gradin would play eight seasons for the Canucks, beginning in 1978. He was almost always the best-conditioned player on the team. On game day, for example, he'd take the morning skate at the Pacific Coliseum before going on at least a 30-minute run near the waters of Burrard Inlet.

Always fit, always ready to play, Gradin proved to be durable and unafraid of the rigours of the NHL.

"The toughest European players I saw in those days were Thomas Gradin and Borje Salming [of the Toronto Maple Leafs], because it seemed everyone in the world took a run at them, figuring

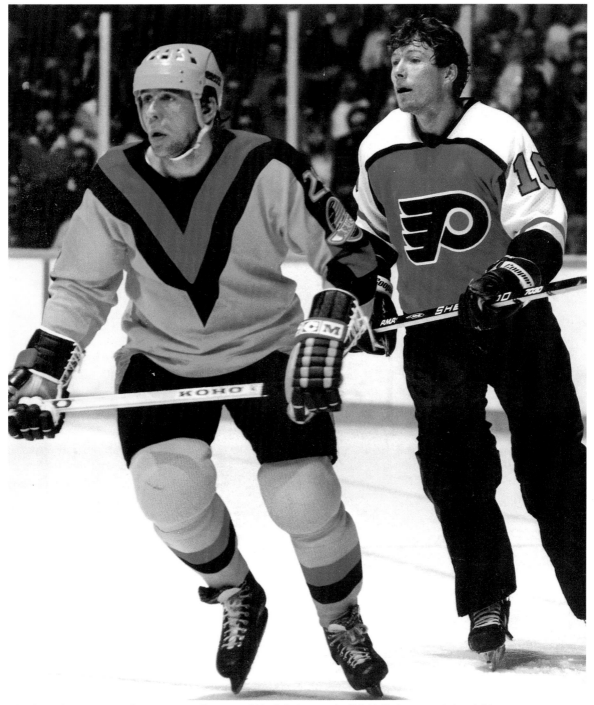

In his Flying-V Canucks uniform, Bubla gets position on Flyers centre Bobby Clarke in an era when Philadelphia players wore the long shell for pants.

Reaching into foreign player markets has been a lifeline for the Canucks in their everlasting quest to claim the Stanley Cup.

Swedish import Lars Lindgren rushes the puck from behind the net.

they were chicken Swedes," Neale says. "Gradin would always play hard, even in Philadelphia, where they always went after him."

Vancouver fans fell in love with their imported players and management obliged them when the Canucks signed Czechoslovakian stars Ivan Hlinka and Jiri Bubla, but only after some clandestine meetings, some on the yacht of owner Frank Griffiths, Sr.

"That was during the Communist regime and those guys were really great players, even though it was late in their careers," says Penny. "Scouts weren't welcome in the Eastern Bloc countries. Mostly you went there as a tourist and booked into

your hotel. You'd go to games appearing like you were on holidays.

"You'd get off a plane in, say, Prague, try to rent a car and get a map. If you didn't know where you were going, you'd try to hire a driver."

Hlinka and Bubla came to Vancouver in 1981 and, along with Gradin, Lindgren and Lars Molin, helped the Canucks reach the playoffs, and then the Stanley Cup Final for the first time.

The Canucks extended their reach in the late 1980s when Canucks general manager Pat Quinn managed to attract Soviet stars Igor Larionov and Vladimir Krutov just before drafting Pavel Bure into the organization.

With a spring in his stride, Igor Larionov was a speedy centreman capable of dancing around opponents.

It was the ever-present Penny who scouted the key international game that made Bure eligible for the NHL Entry Draft in 1989, with the Canucks using the 113th selection to take a Soviet player many NHL teams thought ineligible for the draft.

"In those days, when you were draft eligible in the Soviet Union, you very seldom left the country," Penny says. "I just happened to be in Finland on a scouting trip when the Russian national team was training in a small northern city. On Christmas Day I'm sitting in this out-of-the-way rink and there aren't a lot of people there. Bure played in that game against Finland."

To be eligible for the NHL draft, import players had to play more than 10 games for their team. Penny and the Canucks did the legwork to prove Bure had reached 11.

"We had a friend in Finland named Goran Stubb and he somehow got us the game sheet from that international game to show Bure had played," Penny says. "It counted towards the 11 that made him eligible. What a break. I had borrowed Goran's car to get there and thought I'd just be watching a practice run by [coach] Viktor Tikhonov. Turned out it was a bona fide game that really mattered."

The swashbuckling Bure joined the Canucks in 1991 and was quickly dubbed "The Russian Rocket." Twice he scored 60 goals in a seasons and played in Vancouver's second trip to the Stanley Cup Final in 1994.

Reaching into foreign player markets has been a lifeline for the Canucks in their everlasting quest to claim the Stanley Cup, including the drafting of the Sedin twins, Daniel and Henrik, in 1999.

"That market was out there and God bless Jake Milford for venturing there before other GMs followed suit," adds Penny. "Our roaming around really paid off."

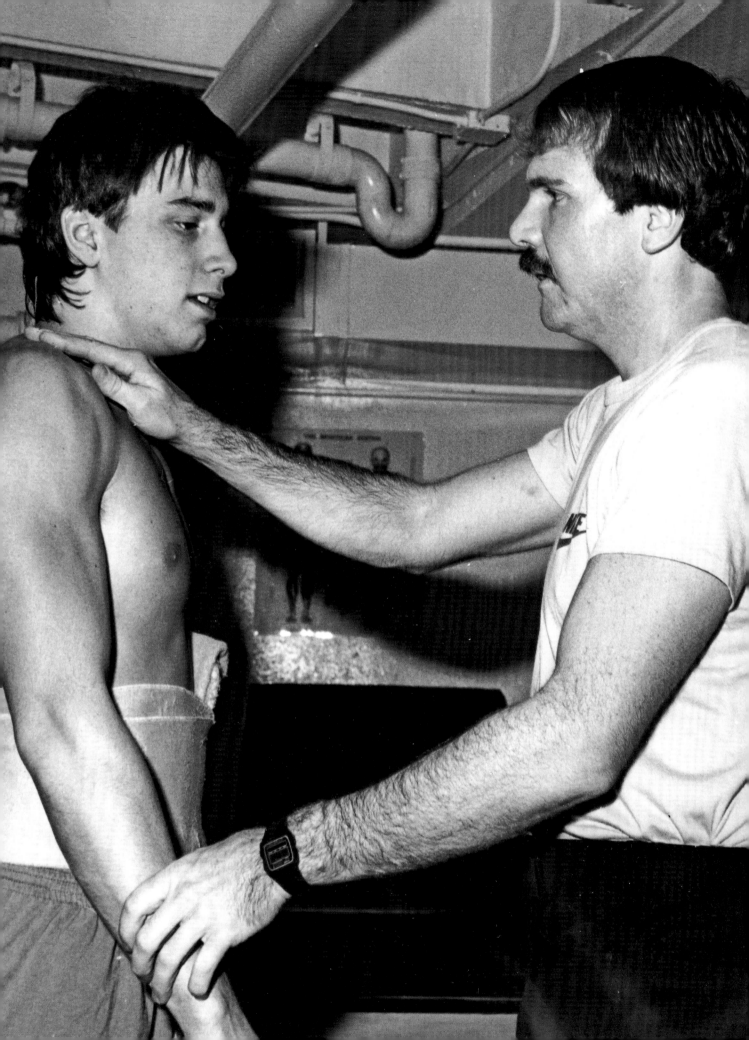

LARRY ASHLEY
Commitment to excellence

LARRY ASHLEY WOULD HAVE BEEN the perfect Texas hold 'em poker player. Quiet. Deep-thinking. Always one step ahead of the opposition.

Ashley was the Canucks' medical trainer for 14 years. He loved his work and loved the people he worked with, from 1981 until his premature passing in September 1995. He succumbed to cancer at the age of 42.

But his memory lives on in so many ways. The Larry Ashley Scholarship Program provides funding assistance for British Columbia students pursuing studies in the fields of sports medicine and athletic training.

Sports medicine and athletic training: Ashley made them his whole world.

Through the Vancouver Canucks Alumni, a major contributor of funds to sustain the scholarship program is the annual Larry Ashley Golf Classic that attracts current and former players not only from the Canucks organization but also throughout the NHL.

Ashley was known league-wide for his passion to continually learn the latest medical advancements within his profession. At his urging, the Canucks became the first sports franchise in North America to use a hyperbaric chamber to treat injuries.

"Larry always had a book in his hand, reading up on the latest medical discoveries," former Canucks trainer, the late Ken Fleger remembered.

Above: Ashley was respected throughout the NHL for his fine work in the training room.

Left: Larry Ashley monitors the condition of Canucks prize rookie Cam Neely at training camp in 1983.

"He would even go into the operating room at the University of British Columbia to watch Dr. Ross Davidson perform surgery. Dr. Davidson was a Canucks team doctor at the time."

Fleger was the Canucks' head trainer in 1981 when he insisted that general manager Harry Neale consider hiring Ashley from the Quebec Nordiques. "I knew Larry wanted out of Quebec and I knew what he was capable of doing in a dressing room, despite his young age," Fleger remembered.

Fleger and Ashley worked the Team Canada bench together during the 1985 World Hockey Championships in Prague, Czechoslovakia, settling for a silver medal when the host team beat Canada 5–3 in the final. Ashley was with Team Canada on two other occasions and also represented the Western Conference in two NHL All Star Games.

"He touched a tremendous number of people," former Canucks equipment manager Gerry Dean says. "That's reflected in the fact he was named president of the Professional Hockey Athletic Trainers Society (PHATS) and also served as president of the NHL Trainers' Association."

Canucks equipment manager Pat O'Neill, who's been in the Vancouver organization for 22 years and has represented Team Canada in several international tournaments (including the 2010 Olympics), worked closely with Ashley. In 1996, O'Neill became the first recipient of the Larry Ashley Award, presented to the trainer or equipment manager in the NHL who best exemplifies the character and commitment to excellence displayed by Ashley throughout his career.

O'Neill summed things up exquisitely when he said: "Being acknowledged in anything associated with Larry Ashley is a great honour. Anyone who ever met the man would agree."

Ashley was inducted into the British Columbia Hockey Hall of Fame in 2006.

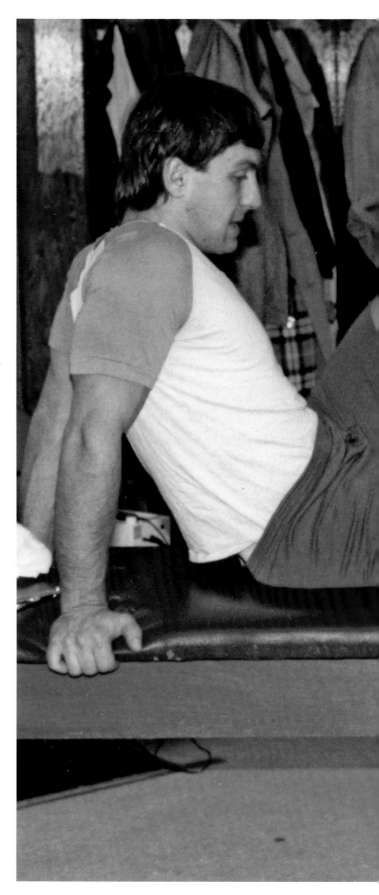

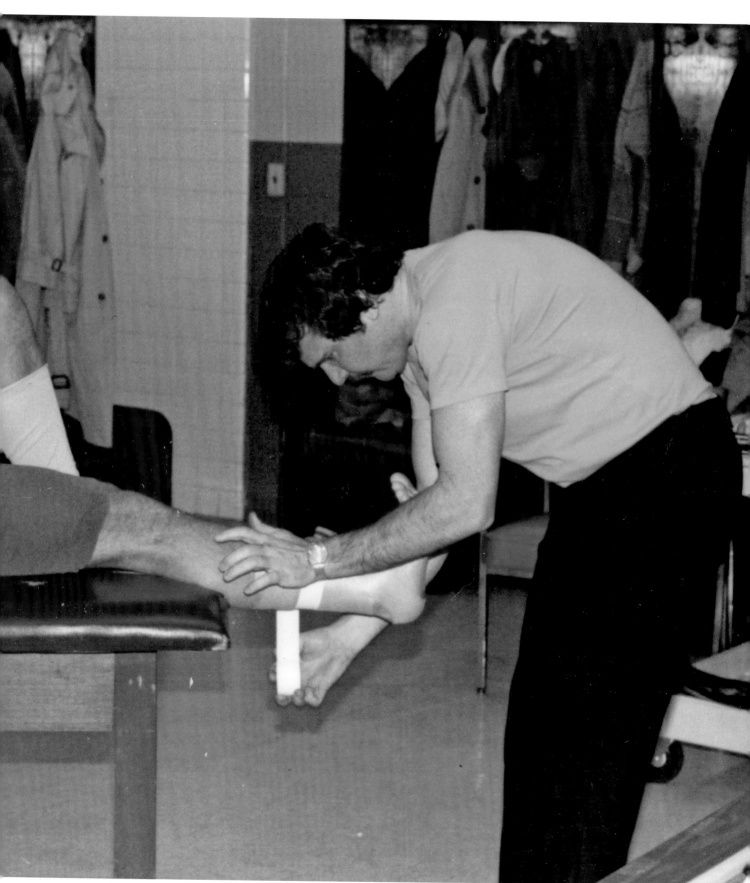

A young Stan Smyl watches the magic performed by the thoughtful Ashley. The training room was Ashley's office and players respected his territory.

DAVE WILLIAMS
"Tiger" did it his way

THE IRREPRESSIBLE DAVE (TIGER) WILLIAMS had never been traded—not even during his rambunctious junior days in Swift Current with the Broncos—when he was suddenly dispatched to the Vancouver Canucks by the Toronto Maple Leafs during the 1980 Lake Placid Olympics.

At first, Williams was hurt and angry. He loved playing for controversial Leafs owner Harold Ballard and had never even considered what it would be like playing for another National Hockey League team.

After all, Williams had it pretty good in Toronto, where his linemates were usually Darryl Sittler and Lanny McDonald. They could put the puck in the net and Williams supplied the sandpaper.

The hardscrabble Williams knew only one way to play—full out and with a take-no-prisoners approach that made him a fan favourite at Maple Leaf Gardens for five-plus seasons. Then his almost perfect world was shattered when he was abruptly swapped to the Canucks, along with Jerry Butler, in a trade that sent Rick Vaive and Bill Derlago to Toronto on February 18, 1980.

Canucks general manager Jake Milford was rolling the dice on this bold move, crossing his fingers that Williams and Butler would provide Vancouver with a new-found sense of security on the combative side of the game. The Canucks were starting to stock their roster with players from

Above: Tiger Williams loved to play for the fans and was willing to sacrifice almost anything in order to give the Canucks a chance for success.

Left: There was never a dull moment when the swashbuckling Williams mixed it up in enemy territory, often changing the complexion of the team, claimed teammate Darcy Rota.

Europe who weren't used to the physical pounding of the NHL.

Williams sucked up his pride and provided the Canucks with what management was looking for, a player who yielded to no other, no matter the circumstances.

"I played the game for the fans," remembers Williams. "I was hard on teammates at times because I believed there should be no passengers. I guess I wore a few guys down, but I always showed up and gave an effort. Fans appreciated that."

Williams gains possession as Canucks captain Stan Smyl prepares to get in position closer to the net. In addition to his toughness, Tiger was no slouch when it came to scoring.

Ride 'em cowboy! Williams jumps on his hockey stick for a celebratory glide after joyously scoring in Maple Leaf Gardens against former teammates from Toronto.

So did most teammates, because Williams raised the bar when it came to putting everything on the line in order to be successful.

"He hated losing, really despised what that represented," teammate Darcy Rota says. "He changed the complexion of our team. Winning was everything to Tiger. He would battle or fight anybody. There were no shortcuts. He wanted to win so badly." In his first full season with Vancouver, the swashbuckling Williams scored a career-high 35 goals during the 1980–81 campaign, and led the NHL in penalty minutes with a whopping 343. Naturally, he was an instant hit at the Pacific Coliseum.

Williams took up residence with his family in West Vancouver and was recognizable from Ambleside to Stanley Park, from the Fraser River to Burrard Inlet. And especially at the Coliseum, where he loved to rock the opposition with old-time hockey.

But deep down, Williams also wanted to play again in Toronto, even for just one game. He got his wish on December 10, 1980, when the Canucks played at Maple Leaf Gardens for the first time since Williams was traded.

Williams marked the occasion by scoring against his former team, then rebelliously riding his hockey stick nearly the length of the ice in celebration.

"The building was full and the greatest thing about the picture of that moment is not me sitting on the stick, but in the background Butsy [Butler] is laughing so hard, leaning over the boards, gloves pretty nearly on the ice," Williams recalls. "It was one of those moments in sports. I had never done that before in my life. I had never seen anybody do it. It just happened.

"It was a tight game until that moment. To play against Mr. Ballard's blue and white, the mighty Leafs, was a big moment in my life.

"After the game, we were sitting in the dressing room and Butsy was looking over at me and we just started laughing. Even Steamer [Stan Smyl] was laughing. He asked me, 'What the heck made you think of doing that?'

"My buddies like Curt Fraser were just flabbergasted. But, you know, it just happened. And the fans, they were awesome. Everywhere I've played, I feel those fans felt that I was their boy. I was the guy that was never going to let them down.

"I know, as a fan myself now, you want to have guys on your team that will never let you down. At the end of the day, you are responsible to the fans, like it or not, because without them, we don't have a game."

Vancouver fans saw Williams score the franchise's first playoff overtime goal on April 8, 1982, at 14:20 for a 2–1 decision to give the Canucks a 2–0 series lead against the arch-rival Calgary Flames.

"Believe it or not, the good thing about being traded is that it's nothing but a plus in your life," he says. "I wish I'd gotten traded 10 times, not five. Everywhere you go, there's a whole new experience. If you stay in the same city your entire career, you only have one dimension on how this game really works.

"In Vancouver, there were some things I didn't like at first because I really do believe in the traditional things. The older guys run the show in my world. It took a while to get that way in Vancouver.

A bouncing puck and a determined Tiger made life difficult for visiting netminders, even with a rival defenceman draped all over the tenacious left winger.

"If you're not willing to die to win, I don't want you on my team."

"We started to get better when the character started to come out of guys like the Smyls, the Frasers and [Harold] Snepsts. You know, if you're not willing to die to win, I don't want you on my team."

Rota recalls joining the Canucks a few weeks earlier than Williams and watched him grow into a respected contributor despite his many on-ice mannerisms that often bordered on the bizarre.

"He was respected in the dressing room because there were no shortcuts," says Rota. "I believe he became a better player in Vancouver, although you were never quite sure what he would do next. He probably would have beaten up his brother if it helped with a game.

"But, you know, he was sly like a fox. He brought his briefcase along to the dressing room and was very bright when it came to investments. He helped a lot of players in that regard."

Williams would have liked to play 1,000 NHL games, but came up just short due to injuries and league-imposed suspensions. His highlights include his first game, his first goal and his first Stanley Cup Final in 1982 with the Canucks.

"The guy up in the stands, the guy that drove through a snow storm to get there, all he wants out of you is an effort," Williams adds. "He doesn't want you to perform a miracle. He just wants you to give it all you've got. I wanted to represent that guy."

"It is a game of mistakes, but if you don't risk something, you're never going to win. You've got to get out to the end of the limb. That's where you'll find the best fruit."

"Every once in a while you fall off, but pick yourself up and get back at it. It's so simple, so clear. That's why I loved playing for [coach] Roger Neilson. He just let you do what you could for the team."

Williams always seemed to be in the middle of the action as he constantly worked hard enough to be a pain in the rear of opposing players like Chicago's Bob Murray.

TOWEL POWER
Coach Neilson introduces a tradition

THE LATE ROGER NEILSON was an innovative and resourceful coach, especially during his 16 seasons behind the benches of eight NHL teams. Some called him colourful, others called him unconventional, still others called him quirky, but everyone agrees that "they broke the mould" when they made Neilson a man who was truly a career coach.

If he wasn't wearing a bag over his head, as Neilson did once in Toronto when he was with the Maple Leafs, he was starting a hockey tradition in Vancouver that spread throughout the NHL.

Neilson reached a milestone 1,000 regular-season games as an NHL head coach, but he is most fondly remembered in Canucks history, not for his 133 regular-season games with the team, but for their 17 playoff games in 1982. Neilson and Ron Smith were assistant coaches to Harry Neale during that 1981–82 season, but Neilson took over as head coach following a late-season league suspension handed to Neale. The players responded with a winning streak heading into the post-season, beat Calgary and Los Angeles in the first two playoff rounds, and even won the first game of the conference final in the intimidating, cathedral-like old Chicago Stadium.

Game 2 and the stage was set for Neilson to cement his place in Canucks folklore May 1, 1982, when Chicago's Denis Savard scored a late power play goal to effectively seal a 4–1 victory.

Above: Roger Neilson was wired for sound from behind the Canucks bench.

Left: The historic towel-waving surrender orchestrated by Roger Neilson from the Vancouver bench during the Stanley Cup playoffs in Chicago.

The often unpredictable Neilson had the Canucks waiting for his next move.

"We were getting whipped," recalls Smith, "and we felt like it was a horribly officiated game by referee Bob Myers. I remember a couple of times earlier when I'd yelled out at Myers, 'We give up, we surrender, we give up.' Then I see Roger holding up a white towel on the end of a hockey stick. Of course, Tiger [Williams] did it, and a few others."

Williams was once quoted as saying, "I asked Roger at the time if we should throw our sticks on the ice." He says Neilson replied, "No, I've done that before. Let's surrender."

Up went the white flag . . . er . . . towel.

Out of the game went Neilson, escorted off the ice by three of his players, including captain Stan Smyl.

"I think a lot of us were surprised by what he did," says Smyl. "Roger was always respectful at the bench and had a controlled bench. This was really an extreme way for him to react to something he wasn't happy about. I remember he apologized to us in the dressing room afterwards, that he didn't want to blow the incident

out of proportion and would let the league deal with it."

Neilson received a heavy fine, but that was the extent of the punishment. It was not, however, the end of the story.

The Canucks returned home from Chicago to a blizzard of white towels. An Air Canada 747 passed the team's United Airlines plane on the tarmac and the pilot was waving a white towel out his window.

The owner of a local T-shirt company, Butts Giraud, seized on the promotion and was selling white towels outside the Pacific Coliseum for Game 3.

Towel Power!

Darcy Rota was a key member of that '82 playoff team, and to this day he believes Neilson's stunt was more calculated than spontaneous.

"I was caught totally off-guard," says Rota, "but history tells me that this is something Roger might have thought about at one time. He always had things pretty well planned out and the result was exactly what Roger wanted. He deflected the loss

Fans in Vancouver picked up on the 1982 White Towel craze that soon became a playoff tradition.

The Canucks returned home from Chicago to a blizzard of white towels.

into something completely different. Instead of being down after the game, all we talked about was the white towels and the coach getting kicked out."

Fuelled by the support of their white towel–waving fans, the Canucks went on to beat Chicago and advance to their first-ever Stanley Cup Final.

Sellout crowds waving white towels! It became a symbol of playoff success.

When they talk of the Roger Neilson legend in Vancouver, he is forever linked to a flimsy piece of white cloth that illustrated the rebellious nature of that Canucks team.

Towel power will always be part of Canucks hockey history, leaving a playoff legacy that has since become commonplace in arenas throughout the NHL.

RICHARD BRODEUR

"King Richard" rules first run to Cup Final

RICHARD BRODEUR NEVER IMAGINED he would become a king in Vancouver, especially when he was told to expect a ticket to minor-league Dallas rather than one to stardom.

Even today, 30 years later, he can clearly recall what Canucks general manager Jake Milford said after he was acquired from the New York Islanders for an exchange of fifth-round picks on October 6, 1980. He was just insurance, Milford said, brought in to play behind incumbent goalies Glen Hanlon and Gary Bromley. Those were the facts of life.

"When I got here, they had Glen Hanlon, who was 'The Franchise,' the young coming goalie, and Gary Bromley," said Brodeur, 28 at the time.

"Jake told me I was labelled to go to the minors. I said to him: 'I just need one chance. Give me one break. Let me show you what I can do.'"

Then fate intervened. The second day Brodeur was in the Canucks camp, Bromley suffered a groin injury. Shortly thereafter, Hanlon hurt his knee. In quick order, Richard Brodeur went from an insurance policy to the starter.

"For six weeks, I was by myself," said the man who would eventually become "King." "I had my shot and I took it and I never let it go."

Brodeur became the Canucks' number-one goalie that season and continued his stellar play through the 1981–82 campaign, eventually leading to a deal that sent Hanlon away to St. Louis.

"Richard was a truly remarkable guy," recalls teammate Darcy Rota. "There was this 5-foot-7, pudgy little guy that could hardly skate, or so it seemed. It was hard to imagine at the time that he would become our most valuable player."

Brodeur wasn't quite the king yet. That would come in the playoffs when the Canucks, a sub-.500 team, managed their magical run to the Stanley Cup Final.

Above: The "pudgy little guy" became the Canucks most valuable player.

Left: King Richard crouches in his familiar stance, zealously guarding the Canucks net.

Canucks centre Ivan Boldirev listens to Brodeur bark orders in the defensive zone.

"We were a real bunch of misfits and characters that jelled together after Harry Neale [the Canucks' head coach] was suspended for that brawl in Quebec City," Brodeur said. "We never lost another game after that and we were hot going into the playoffs. We believed in ourselves."

And the fans began to believe in their "King." After the Canucks dispatched the Calgary Flames in three straight in a best-of-five first round, the Los Angeles Kings were next.

"We were in the warm-up and Stan Smyl came up to me and said: 'Did you see the sign the fan over there has? It says "King Richard." That's you,'" Brodeur explained. "After the game, I asked what was going on with that. They told me that after we beat Calgary, Tom Larscheid was talking on the

radio about the next series with L.A. and he said: 'The Kings are coming in but we don't care because we have our own king, King Richard.'

"So it started there and it stuck. We beat L.A. and we kept going and the name King Richard has stuck for all these years. All my buddies still call me King."

The Canucks took out both the Kings and Chicago Blackhawks in five games before they ran headlong into the New York Islander dynasty led by Denis Potvin, Bryan Trottier, Mike Bossy and Billy Smith. The Canucks went down four straight in the '82 Final.

"The Islanders were an unbelievable team," Brodeur said. "We weren't that far away, maybe one player, a sniper like Mike Bossy. I was very fortunate

Brodeur always enjoyed the ride during his NHL hey-days.

"You'd never see Richard blame a teammate when we were scored on. He just went about his way, having fun all the time."

that I won a Memorial Cup and an Avco Cup with the [WHA] Quebec Nordiques, but those playoffs were probably the greatest time of my life."

The Canucks desperately needed a razor-sharp Brodeur in those series because injuries decimated the defence. Vancouver went 6-0-3 down the stretch, only to have defenceman Kevin McCarthy break an ankle just before playoffs. Brodeur gave the Canucks the confidence they needed in the post-season.

"What a good teammate he was," Rota says. "He was kind of ho-hum at times, but that was his way of dealing with pressure. We got on a roll because he was even-keeled in his approach to business.

"He was so much different than Tony Esposito when I played with him in Chicago. They were both great competitors, great goalies, but in different ways. Tony was an outgoing, brash kind of guy, while Richard was just happy-go-lucky. You'd never see Richard blame a teammate when we were

scored on. He just went about his way, having fun all the time."

Brodeur was 29 that spring. He had perspective. He was no longer a young pro on his way up. He knew what was happening might never happen again—and that turned out to be the case.

"When you're young, you sometimes just go day by day, you enjoy the ride and you have fun," Brodeur explained. "But when you've been around for a while, you realize those chances don't come too often . . . to make an impression in the playoffs and to go far and have a shot at winning the Stanley Cup.

"So I enjoyed every moment. I savoured it. Even now, it is my greatest accomplishment. I mean, how many times do you have a shot at making a name for yourself?"

Indeed. How often can a man arrive as a minor leaguer and leave as a king?

COLIN CAMPBELL
Saving his best for the playoffs

IT'S A RARE OCCASION WHEN A SCRAPPY, physical defenceman who didn't register a single goal during the regular season becomes a significant post-season scorer—for one game at least.

That's exactly what happened to Colin Campbell when he scored twice in a playoff game, including the overtime winner during the Vancouver Canucks magnificent 1982 run to the Stanley Cup Final. And, no one was more surprised than Richard Brodeur, the Canucks brilliant netminder, who was more used to having Campbell block shots than score goals.

Brodeur chuckles to this day about Campbell's unexpected heroics during a time when the Canucks had many unsung heroes step up their efforts in the playoffs, much to the liking of their netminder.

"In practice, when Colie lined up with the guys along the blueline to take shots, I'd take my (catching) glove off and tease him, saying I could stop his shot with my bare hand," remembers Brodeur. "He'd just laugh and laugh, and shoot at my head.

"He was a great character and I loved having him in front of me. There was nothing fancy about him, just get the puck out of our zone. He was very strong and he had no fear. Colie contributed when it mattered."

The stocky defender did manage to score four overtime goals over the years in the post-season,

Above: Campbell was noted for his defensive prowess, although one of his proudest moments came in the post-season when he suddenly became a timely scorer.

Left: There was a serious side to Colin Campbell, as shown here, but the stocky blueliner kept his teammates in stitches with his unique sense of humour.

though, and retained the puck from the last one as a souvenir that he still cherishes.

Campbell likes to joke about how he scored a goal for the Canucks just 23 seconds into overtime on April 18, 1982, against the Los Angeles Kings at the Fabulous Forum, giving Vancouver a 4–3 victory and a 2–1 series lead in the second round of the playoffs.

Campbell keeps eyes on teammate Thomas Gradin (23) to avoid trouble behind the Canucks net.

The unlikely hero scored his first goal of the season during regulation time that night to take some of the pressure off scoring stars Thomas Gradin, Ivan Boldirev and Ivan Hlinka, plus the always steady Brodeur. Scoring a second goal was even more of a shock.

For the hard-as-nails Campbell, the goal had significant meaning because he'd missed almost half the games during the 1981–82 season with a knee injury. He remembers being in the hospital after surgery, along with a teammate, when they were joined by another member of the organization, Arthur Griffiths, youngest son of owner Frank Griffiths, Sr.

Young Arthur had hurt his knee in a ski accident, and as a result Campbell and the Canucks soon got a new knee-strengthening machine in the team's training room so that everyone could rehab

their injuries with the most modern equipment of the day.

Campbell recalls that he got back into the lineup late in the regular season, and just in time, it turned out. Injuries sidelined defencemen Rick Lanz, Jiri Bubla and Kevin McCarthy with the playoffs just around the corner.

"We survived because we had a tough team with a lot of character," remembers Campbell. "No one was going to push us around. In the first playoff game against Calgary, it took only eight seconds before Curt Fraser pounded on Willi Plett [of the Flames], which was fine with me. I'd already fought him four times that season.

"Roger Neilson was behind the bench in the playoffs because our head coach was suspended for an incident that happened in Quebec. Harry Neale had already done a good job of establishing

Campbell maintains his defensive position, stick on ice and focused on the play, while zealously defending the Vancouver goal.

"We survived because we had a tough team with a lot of character," remembers Campbell. "No one was going to push us around."

a working relationship with the players and Roger continued in that direction. We found ways to win."

The Canucks dispatched Calgary in three straight in the first round of the playoffs, but then Vancouver split the first two games at home against Los Angeles in the second round, meaning the Canucks would need at least one win in Los Angeles in the best-of-seven series.

They got both games, winning 4–3 on Campbell's overtime goal and 5–4 the next game. The Canucks took Game 5 in Vancouver 5–2 to win the series 4–1 and move into the conference final against Chicago.

"The funny thing about those goals in Los Angeles is that on the first one I shot, it went into

the net off the behind of their defenceman, Jerry Korab," says Campbell. "The second, I didn't see it after I shot. Ivan Hlinka won the draw, got it back to me at the point. I just shot and started to retreat, hoping that I wouldn't give up a two-on-one rush if it was blocked. It wasn't.

"Hlinka joked later he got the draw to me fast because he wanted the game to end quickly so he could have a cigarette."

Campbell finally earned a Stanley Cup ring in 1994, ironically against the Canucks when he was an assistant coach with the New York Rangers. He later joined the National Hockey League head office, rising to senior executive vice-president and director of hockey operations.

RON DELORME
Teammates came first

RON DELORME WAS HELD in high esteem by teammates during his five seasons as a rugged winger for the Vancouver Canucks because he could read a situation and react accordingly.

Above: Delorme played the role of a bodyguard when teammates needed his presence.

Left: Long and lean, Ron Delorme fought many of the NHL tough guys, including Chicago's Grant Mulvey.

Like on the night of May 6, 1982, when the Canucks were putting the finishing touches on the Chicago Blackhawks in Game 5 of the Campbell Conference championship. The Canucks dominated the spirited contest at Chicago Stadium, winning 6–2 to advance to the Stanley Cup Final for the first time. But not before Delorme showed his mettle when he engaged Grant Mulvey in a lively battle after Mulvey had tried to take advantage of Vancouver defenceman Lars Lindgren during a line change in the third period.

Video of the fight can still be found on the Internet and shows Delorme holding off the bigger Mulvey while throwing a series of right hands that opened a nasty gash over Mulvey's left eye, leaving the white jersey of the Chicago gladiator soaked in blood.

Delorme had many a battle during his 524-game NHL career, but none as storied as when he bloodied the bully Mulvey. Delorme dressed for 15 playoff games that spring, assisted on two goals and was assessed 31 minutes in penalties. He was a situational player, for sure, and just as valuable as role players like Gary Lupul and Gerry Minor.

The Canucks had a tightly knit team that season, a group that came together following a brawl in Quebec City that resulted in a 10-game suspension for Canucks coach Harry Neale and elevated assistant Roger Neilson into the head coach position.

Delorme, normally a right winger, faces off with St. Louis Blues centre Doug Wickenheiser.

"We all knew we weren't a great team, talent-wise," says Delorme. "But we were certainly a team in terms of togetherness. The camaraderie was unbelievable. It was the team unison that got us to the Final.

"So much of the credit went to Roger Neilson because he made everybody feel so important. Everybody was equal. At least that's the way he made you feel."

Delorme recalls suffering an ankle injury and going into the medical room for treatment. He was waiting for trainer Larry Ashley to finish working on star centre Thomas Gradin when Neilson entered the room.

"He asked me how I was doing," recalls Delorme. "I told him how sore I was and was barely able to walk. He proceeded to tell me that I had to dress and sit on the bench, even though I couldn't play. The other team had to believe that I was okay. He walked out of the room without even asking how Thomas was. That's the way he was and the entire team would have gone to the wall for Roger Neilson."

Delorme was used to going to the wall for his teams, especially the Canucks. He had accumulated 177 minutes in penalties during the regular season in 1981–82 and knew his job was to protect teammates, to provide a deterrent when the occasion called for an enforcer.

The Chicago series was a physical battle from the start. Chicago had players like Al Secord and Mulvey, to name two, who tried to run the Canucks out of the rink. It didn't work. The Canucks stood up to the challenge, especially Delorme, Harold Snepsts, Tiger Williams, Stan Smyl, Curt Fraser, Darcy Rota, Colin Campbell and Doug Halward.

By the fifth game, when the Blackhawks knew their season was just about over, tempers got the better of some players, including Mulvey.

The Canucks had matched up defencemen Snepsts and Lindgren whenever Chicago star Denis Savard was on the ice. The strategy worked magnificently, with Vancouver's backup netminder Rick Heinz always signalling Neilson with his catching glove when Heinz thought Savard was going out on the next shift.

Delorme keeps his spirits (and stick) high while in the company of the Winnipeg Jets.

"Roger always found a way to get the players he wanted on the ice against Savard," Delorme recalls. "Roger always did the little things that most people didn't notice that meant a lot to us in terms of strategy. He had us believing it would work."

Delorme also believes that Chicago coach Bob Pulford purposely sent Mulvey on the ice to try to change the game. Mulvey came from the bench and cross-checked Lindgren in the face during a line change.

"He was doing his job, without being told what to do," Delorme says. "I happened to be on the ice at the time and I just shot over there and wanted to get at Mulvey.

"We went at it and a line brawl broke out. I got the best of him, then asked, 'What were you doing?' He told me he just wanted to change the direction of the game. Then he snuck in a punch and I got mad. I pounded him until you could tell

he wanted me to stop. It was a gentlemen's agreement, so I did."

Role player and team player. Delorme was always there for others, no matter the consequences.

It's Delorme's belief the Canucks also grew as a team during a regular-season game in Edmonton from an incident involving Dave Semenko of the Oilers. Semenko was the bodyguard for rising star Wayne Gretzky and in that particular game went after the always antagonistic Williams.

"I stepped in and suddenly Semenko hit me right in the eye," Delorme says. "I wasn't expecting it because I thought we were going to back off. He hit me so hard that he gave me a black eye and rung my bell.

"I remember seeing lights. I told him to hang on because I couldn't see. Then we went at it but good. After the game, Harry Neale made a speech like you wouldn't believe about the things I was doing for the team. We might have got beaten that game [5–3 on March 13], but we went on to play well after that, winning most of our games before the playoffs."

Delorme had to stop fighting for a few games, though, because he hurt his hand in a bout with Washington defenceman Rick Green. In fact, Delorme was in the stands watching in Quebec the night a fan took a poke at Williams and Neale went after the fan, leading to his suspension.

Born in North Battleford, Saskatchewan, Delorme trained for the NHL by playing junior in the Western Canada Hockey League for Swift Current and then Lethbridge, where the Broncos franchise was relocated.

The Kansas City Scouts selected Delorme in the fourth round of the 1975 NHL amateur draft. He also was picked in the third round of the World Hockey Association draft and spent his first pro year in the rival WHA with the Denver Spurs and the Ottawa Civics.

His grim determination was always evident as Delorme knew how to play his role.

"I've been through three changes in logos and I always make a joke that I've got three tattoos, one for every logo," says Delorme.

Delorme got to the NHL with the Colorado Rockies in 1976 and was claimed on waivers by Vancouver in 1981. After a nine-year career ended with a knee injury, Delorme became a scout for the Canucks and rose to the position of chief amateur scout.

He once told the *Vancouver Sun* that he would "forever be a Canucks."

"I've been through three changes in logos and I always make a joke that I've got three tattoos, one for every logo," says Delorme.

He's long been a role model for aspiring First Nations players and athletes and he was instrumental in the drafting of Gino Odjick, another native player who would rise in popularity with Canucks fans for his aggressive approach to the game.

"I made a strong push for Odjick based upon what our need for the team was at the time [1990]," recalls Delorme. "There was a need for someone like that. I didn't know that he would become a much better player than people gave him credit for. He was smart enough to know that if he looked after people like Pavel Bure, he would get more playing time."

Delorme likes to remind people that he produced a 20-goal season in the NHL with Colorado in 1978–79 and scored 83 NHL goals in all. His only NHL post-season goal came with Vancouver in 1984.

Delorme was more than just a mucker and grinder during an NHL career that spans five decades as player and scout. In the Canucks organization, he's considered the ultimate team player.

JOHN GARRETT

Unlikely all-star almost upstaged The Great One

IN THE CATEGORY OF "TRUTH is often stranger than fiction," John Garrett played in an NHL All Star Game representing the Vancouver Canucks without garnering even a single vote in the selection process—in either conference he played in—and was nearly named most valuable player.

He did it after playing just one full game for the Canucks. Garrett had been acquired from the Quebec Nordiques on February 4, 1983, to become back-up to Vancouver's number-one starter, ("King") Richard Brodeur.

Harry Neale was the Vancouver general manager of the day. He wanted a veteran presence on hand, just in case something happened to Brodeur, the superb netminder who had almost single-handedly taken the Canucks to the Stanley Cup Final in the spring of 1982. The price tag to acquire the journeyman Garrett was defenceman Anders Eldebrink.

Vancouver had just lost 7-1 in Montreal to the mighty Canadiens when the trade for Garrett was completed. He was scheduled to back up the durable Brodeur when the Canucks played February 5 against the Maple Leafs in Toronto.

That's where the unexpected trip to the NHL All Star Game on February 8 at Nassau County Coliseum in Uniondale, N.Y., began to unfold.

"The way it worked out, I had my mask painted right away because the guy that did it happened

Above: Garrett was an unlikely NHL All Star Game participant in 1983 and can still laugh about it.

Left: John Garrett focuses on the action as he moves to monitor the puck in the defensive zone.

to live in Toronto," Garrett recalls. "So I had my Canucks mask and was prepared to sit on the bench.

"So I'm sitting there watching the game and Richard's playing. Dan Daoust comes down and there's like five minutes left in the game and he wires a shot that hits Richard right in the mask. He turned a little and it hit him in the ear. It broke his ear drum. So he was out."

Thus the player whom teammates and opponents often called "Cheech" because of his resemblance to moustachioed actor Cheech Marin, made his Canucks debut, mopping up a 6–4 loss. With Brodeur on the sideline, Garrett played again the next night in New Jersey, where Vancouver tied the Devils 4–4 and went into the short all star break with a 17–26–11 record.

But, instead of gathering up his family and heading for new digs in Vancouver, Garrett was off to Long Island, home of the New York Islanders, for the NHL All Star Game, replacing the injured Brodeur.

Every NHL team had to have a representative in the NHL All Star Game, where the eastern Wales Conference team played the Campbell Conference team from the west, and Brodeur was the only Vancouver player named to the team.

"There really wasn't any outstanding goalie in the west that year, with Murray Bannerman from Chicago the other Campbell goalie for the NHL All Star Game," remembers Garrett. "That's how I got into the NHL All Star Game, without gaining a vote in either conference.

"The Canuck players joked about it before I left for Long Island, saying how I played one [full] game and they made me an all-star. I told them that if I won the car for being the most valuable player, we'd sell the car and split the money. We all had a good laugh about it."

Vancouver coach Roger Neilson just happened to be the all-star coach for the Campbell Conference and he determined that Bannerman should be the starter, with Garrett to enter the game midway through the second period.

The Campbell Conference had four rising stars from the Edmonton Oilers (defenceman Paul Coffey and forwards Wayne Gretzky, Jari Kurri and Mark Messier), who were determined to illustrate how the west was on the rise after the Wales Conference had won six of the previous seven NHL All Star Games, including a 4–3 decision in 1977 at the Pacific Coliseum.

Garrett entered the game in the middle of the second period with the score tied 2–2. Dave Babych of the Winnipeg Jets and Dino Ciccarelli

Canucks defender Rick Lanz provides protection for Garrett.

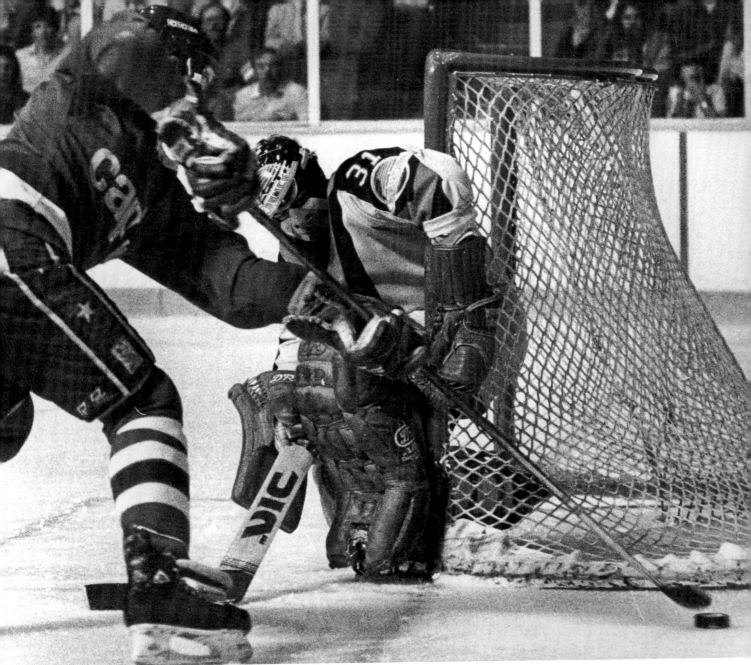

Garrett hugs the goal post and gets ready to block a pass against the Washington Capitals.

of the Minnesota North Stars had scored for the Campbell Conference against netminder Pete Peeters of the Boston Bruins. Michel Goulet of the Nordiques and Ray Bourque of the Bruins had beaten Bannerman.

Now the game got really interesting for Garrett, who had never thought about anything so outrageous as a most valuable player award.

"I made a few saves in the second period and we went ahead 3–2 when Tom McCarthy [of the Minnesota North Stars] scored on Pelle Lindbergh [of the Philadelphia Flyers]," Garrett says. "You could tell it was a game that the guys from the Campbell really wanted to win. It was a matter of

pride because they had been beaten so often by the easterners. All those Edmonton guys, especially Gretzky, wanted to prove that they were better than the older guys from the east.

"So we were cruising along in the third and I'm thinking things are going pretty good. Lanny McDonald [of the Calgary Flames] started telling me that I might win the car, that I already had one of the tires. Every save, he'd come back and tap my pads, telling me I'd got another tire. Then the steering wheel, the glove compartment."

Then along came Gretzky to put an end to the unlikely scenario. All he did was score four goals in the third period to make sure the Campbell

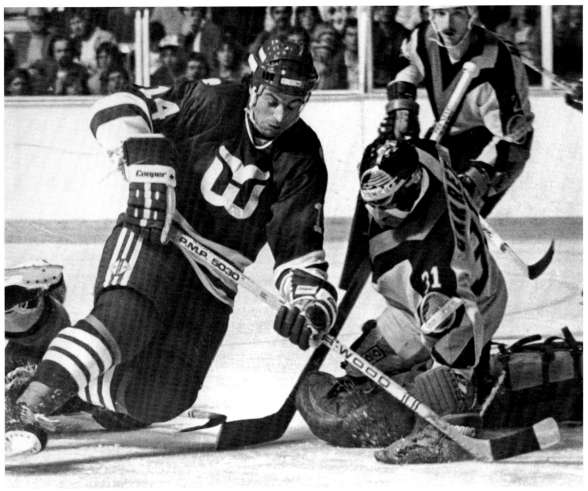

Garrett has the puck in his possession against the Hartford Whalers attack.

"Lanny came back to our net and said something like, 'Oh, oh, there goes the car.'"

Conference won 9–3, thus earning MVP honours—and the car.

Garrett only allowed one goal in half a game, with Don Maloney of the New York Rangers scoring at 14:04 of the third period, assisted by Hector Marini of the Islanders.

Gretzky became the first player in NHL All Star Game history to score four times, a record since equalled by Mario Lemieux in 1990, Vincent Damphousse in 1991, Mike Gartner in 1993 and Dany Heatley in 2003.

"I remember after Wayne's third goal, Lanny came back to our net and said something like, 'Oh, oh, there goes the car,' and later I heard they

had to re-do the MVP voting after Wayne scored his fourth goal," Garrett says. "It was a lot of fun playing with those guys. The young Oilers were just so good, with such a swagger about them. And that was before they started winning all those championships.

"It was a running joke in our dressing room when someone would ask, 'How did you get here?' 'Oh, Air Canada.' Yeah, but it was fun to win, for sure."

When Garrett finally got to Vancouver and rejoined the Canucks, teammates were quick to tell him that Gretzky had taken the car right out of his driveway.

KIRK McLEAN

Shutout earns standing ovation at the Forum

KIRK MCLEAN WAS IN A LEAGUE OF HIS OWN as an NHL goaltender the night he received a standing ovation from the in-the-know crowd at the Montreal Forum that had come to show appreciation for their beloved Montreal Canadiens, not the visiting Vancouver Canucks.

It's not that the Habs faithful hadn't shown respect for opposing players before, just that they hadn't quite grasped that an upstart expansion team like the Canucks could compete at their level.

McLean helped prove they could with a magnificent, 43-save performance that produced a 3-0 Vancouver victory. His good pal Greg Adams supplied the scoring with a hat trick.

The performance signalled that the Canucks were on the verge of arriving as a team to be reckoned with, especially when the shutout was on the road against an Original Six team with more Stanley Cup championships than any other team.

The evening of December 4, 1991, should also be remembered as one of the greatest goaltending performances in the team's history. McLean would go on to show his mettle a few years later with an outstanding 1994 post-season, when the Canucks reached the Stanley Cup Final.

But first, he had proven again that Canucks general manager Pat Quinn was astute in his player analysis when he traded popular Patrik Sundstrom

Above: McLean was known as Captain Kirk to Canucks fans because of his ability to play his best games when it meant the most.

Left: An even-keeled Kirk McLean refused to allow the opposition to rattle him at the toughest of times.

McLean was considered a stand-up goaltender who made many glove-hand saves, but he also relied on his quick feet to make pad and toe stops on shots he couldn't reach with his gloves.

to the New Jersey Devils in 1987 for McLean and Adams. For a team to rise above mediocrity, it had to have a reliable netminder.

McLean proved to be just that, a stand-up goaltender who relied on positioning and quick feet in making the saves that produced wins.

He remembers the Montreal shutout came against a stacked Habs team that included standouts such as goaltender Patrick Roy, centre Guy Carbonneau, defenceman Eric Desjardins and right winger Mike Keane, as the Canadiens were building for their run to the 1993 Stanley Cup title.

"That was quite a game, a really cool occasion," says McLean. "I ended up getting first star and they gave me the standing ovation, which was kind of thrilling, to be quite honest.

"That game in particular showed we could beat one of the best teams and we went on quite a run for the next few years. We would be right up there for a while, fighting for the President's Trophy as the league's top team [in the regular season]."

McLean was the cornerstone of the Canucks for several years as he quietly went about his business. Teammates sometimes called him by the nickname "Weird," remembers Garry Valk, insisting there was nothing unusual about McLean other than his desire to avoid controversy.

"Kirk lasted a long time in a really tough hockey market," says Valk.

"He was so reserved and even-keeled, respected by everyone. You could never tell if he'd let in a bad goal because he wouldn't let it get to him. He never blamed his defencemen. Look at who his best friends were—Dana Murzyn and Dave Babych. It speaks about how good a person he is.

"He never turned around and slammed his stick on the ice after a goal. He was patient because he was such a good skater, could read the play well and had great hands, just an incredible touch with the puck.

"Basically, he was quiet and not really superstitious like most goalies. I don't remember him ever going after a ref if he got bumped, or elbowing somebody in front of our net."

Canucks coach Bob McCammon appreciated McLean's behaviour, especially his ability to never get too excited, and figures that's why McLean was so effective when games were on the line.

"He's kind of a private guy and, for a goalie, pretty normal," McCammon says. "He was very well liked and never stepped out of line. One of his best friends was Trevor Linden, which tells you something about the individual. He had a terrific career."

McLean never envisioned, when he was a young pro in the New Jersey organization, that he would one day be a member of the Canucks. He knew little about Vancouver after playing junior for the Oshawa Generals and being drafted by the Devils in 1984.

He was from Willowdale, a suburb of Toronto. His trade to Vancouver came on September 15, 1987, one of the first deals made by Lou Lamoriello, who had replaced Max McNab as general manger in New Jersey. The Devils were deep in goaltenders

A bevy of goalies in New Jersey made McLean available to Vancouver in a deal orchestrated by Canucks general manager Pat Quinn.

"That game in particular showed we could beat one of the best teams and we went on quite a run for the next few years."

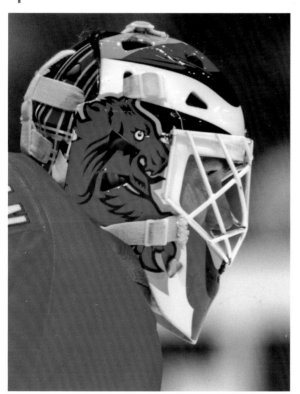

McLean looked forward to his visits to the Montreal Forum and Maple Leaf Gardens in Toronto.

with an organization that included Chris Terreri, Craig Billington, Alain Chevrier and Sean Burke, so McLean was deemed expendable.

McLean had a strange feeling about heading west and knew that his dad would have to listen to his games on radio late at night, if possible, instead of seeing him play in person.

His father wasn't at the Montreal game that produced the standing ovation a few years later, but McLean did have plenty of friends at the rink who had driven over from Toronto to see him play. His performance and steady play thereafter would lead to McLean being revered and dubbed "Captain Kirk" by Vancouver fans.

"Whenever you went into Toronto or Montreal, those Original Six rinks, it was always a big thrill," McLean says. "The Forum was magical, as was Maple Leaf Gardens. Those cities just smell

Great glove save by McLean leaves teammate Doug Lidster looking on in disbelief, with a sigh of relief.

As easy as one-two-three, McLean demonstrates his technique in deflecting a shot out of harm's way.

of hockey. There's snow on the ground. You have that old-school feel and when you finally step on the ice surface, it's just an amazing feeling."

McLean prepared for the game as he always did, participating in the morning skate, having a pre-game meal and taking a nap at the hotel.

"Once you're at the rink, you get that calm feeling because usually the butterflies are before you get there. Once you get to the rink, everything goes away. You're in your home.

"I don't remember too much about the shutout other than the standing ovation was something else. It's one of those nights when you're just in a zone and it just happens for you. You're reacting and making saves, then totally forget about the game."

As a youth, McLean developed a stand-up style that served him well. He admired the play of former stars Bernie Parent and Jacques Plante, and patterned his style after them. McLean could do the butterfly that would later become popular, going down to his knees to use his leg pads to block low shots, but preferred to stay upright on his skates, positioning himself for a reactionary move once a shooter showed his cards.

He learned more about the stand-up style from goaltending coaches Dean Dorsey and Ian Young. McLean stayed with it his entire career, which ended in 2001 with the New York Rangers when he could no longer continue due to aching knees.

"I learned to hold my ground as long as I could and stay with the play," he says. "If a shooter tried to deke, you could use a backward motion to get into some kind of leg save. You made skate saves, toe saves, that kind of stuff, all the time."

McLean made a remarkable stop on Calgary's Robert Reichel in Game 7 of the first round of the 1994 playoffs that kept the overtime game dead-locked and led to Pavel Bure scoring for Vancouver in the second period of sudden death.

McLean posted four shutouts in those play-offs, including consecutive games against Toronto, plus had another absolutely brilliant game in the opener of the Stanley Cup Final against the New York Rangers.

"In the end, we missed the ultimate goal, winning the Cup, and we were that close in seven games," he says. "But I'm happy with my career, other than I didn't finish it in Vancouver."

McLean represented Vancouver in two mid-season NHL All Star Games and was a Second Team NHL All Star in 1992. He was also runner-up to Montreal's Patrick Roy in voting for the Vezina Trophy in 1992 as the league's top netminder.

"It was a good time to play and I was lucky enough to play in 17 NHL seasons, despite two knee operations," he adds. "And that game in Montreal, I may not recall all the details, but I do the ovation. I'm thankful for so many good memories."

McLean became an active member of the Canucks alumni, taking a leadership role in various charity activities throughout British Columbia.

GINO ODJICK
Warrior proud of his heritage

IT WAS A BELIEVE-IT-OR-NOT moment when an enforcer, of all people, managed to score the sixth penalty-shot goal in the history of the Vancouver Canucks.

Successfully converting that showdown was rugged Gino Odjick, primarily a checker and protector of teammates, rather than more illustrious Canucks of the time such as Trevor Linden, Cliff Ronning or Greg Adams.

In fact, Adams had been unsuccessful on the three previous penalty shots awarded the Canucks in 1989.

The popular Odjick, dubbed the "Maniwaki Mauler" due to his reputation for defending his heritage and his fellow Canucks, managed the feat on October 19, 1991, against Calgary Flames netminder Mike Vernon.

The Canucks won 5–2 that evening at the Pacific Coliseum and the talk of the town was Odjick, playing his second pro season. He had amassed 296 penalty minutes as a rookie and scored seven times. His second season resulted in four goals and 348 minutes, the latter a club record at the time.

"It was a warrior thing," Odjick proclaims years later. "You look right and shoot left. Well, I looked right, shot left."

Odjick played just over seven full seasons with the Canucks, fought often and always scored with the fans for his bravery. He produced 47 of his 64 NHL goals for the Canucks, none more memorable than the successful penalty shot against arch-rival Calgary.

Early in the game, Odjick recalls, he detected Flames star defenceman Al MacInnis frequently pinching inside the Vancouver zone.

Above: Odjick was serious when it came to protecting his Canucks teammates.

Left: Gino Odjick learned early in his NHL career to keep his eyes on the business at hand and hold his head high.

Odjick soon proved he could not only fight with the NHL's best, but could also score goals, especially when he had Pavel Bure as a linemate, or was taking a penalty shot.

"I decided to go behind him and got a semi-breakaway," says Odjick. "He hooked me and, in those days, it seemed a tough player would never get a call against a player like MacInnis. But, it was the third time that game, so I guess the referee felt enough was enough."

Odjick made the most of his unexpected opportunity when he beat Vernon with a clean shot. "I buried it. I kept it simple, stupid."

Odjick was always proud that he had improved his game enough as a youngster to make it to the NHL after playing junior in Quebec for the Laval Titan. He lacked confidence at times, but managed to survive by using his warrior instincts. He was drafted 86th overall (fifth round) by the Canucks after being scouted by Vancouver staffer Ron Delorme, also of First Nations heritage.

Not surprisingly, Odjick was hardly prepared for the pro game at first. He was a plodding skater, but tough as nails, remembers Garry Valk, a teammate both in the minors and with the Canucks.

"I believe he was fined for being late for nine of his first 10 practices," says Valk. "With a little guidance he soon figured things out. Everyone loved him when he got to Vancouver, even Geoff Courtnall. Gino picked on him in the dressing room. Gino loved to joke and clown around with the guys.

"He had such a flair for the dramatic. He was always yelling at guys in practice to feed him the puck so he could unleash his first-timer. And he was street smart—smart enough to become friends with our best player, Pavel Bure."

The unsure Odjick began the 1990–91 season in the minors with the Milwaukee Admirals, playing 17 games before he was called up by Vancouver. He knew what his job would be when he played his first NHL game on November 21 at the Coliseum against the Chicago Blackhawks.

"I was in my apartment the night before with my roommate, Shawn Antoski, when I got a call from the Milwaukee GM," recalls Odjick. "I was told I was being called up on an emergency basis. I never came back.

"I knew Vancouver had been pushed around the game before, so I figured I had two choices. I could do my job in Vancouver and earn $110,000 a year, or not do my job and get $30,000 in Milwaukee. I figured out in my brief time in Milwaukee you could barely get by on $30,000. I knew what I had to do with the Canucks. I was willing to do it."

Odjick credits Canucks general manager Pat Quinn, who would take over from Bob McCammon as head coach later in the season, for instilling confidence in a raw rookie.

"When I met Pat Quinn that first day in the NHL, I was walking with my head down," Odjick says. "He was the first non-Native person to tell me to 'lift my head and be proud of who I was.' That was huge. He was like a dad to me, and to all the core group. Nobody came into our house and made the law. We made the law. The Pacific Coliseum was our house."

Odjick recalls Mike Keenan being the Chicago coach at the time and that the Blackhawks believed they were going to push the Canucks around. Never happened.

Odjick enjoyed the lifestyle that came with employment in the NHL.

Odjick fought Chicago ruffians Stu Grimson and Dave Manson in his NHL debut.

"As long as Pat Quinn was around, nobody pushed us around. We had the warriors to go to war. No one had to tell us to fight. We knew our jobs."

Odjick fought Chicago ruffians Stu Grimson and Dave Manson in his NHL debut. He almost had a third scrap, but it was more pushing and shoving as Odjick showed his mettle. "Nobody got hurt, so it wasn't a fight," recalls Odjick.

Canuck fans would chant "Gino, Gino, Gino" when they thought an opponent deserved to be singled out by Odjick. One creative fan brought a sign to the Coliseum that read, "Gino, it's Miller time," in reference to Los Angeles Kings thug Jay Miller.

"I was taught that once the game is over, it's not my job to be a bully," Odjick says. "All I wanted to do was win, to earn my living. To win, you have to make sure all your teammates feel comfortable. I'd look around the dressing room and, if the guys were nervous, you'd want to make them secure. We had one heck of a group for a few years in Vancouver.

"My popularity with fans? I don't know what to say. I was no better than any other player, but no worse either. Pat Quinn made me lift my head up and my spirit walks with him. First Nations people have lots of respect for the Vancouver Canucks. The Canucks and Pat Quinn gave me an opportunity. I never quit. I never backed down."

PAVEL BURE

"Russian Rocket" had hands as fast as his feet

Above: The dashing Bure electrified Canucks fans with his astounding ability to make plays at high speed.

Left: Bure had a powerful stride that allowed him to gather speed and keep the opposition off balance during his spectacular offensive outbursts.

HE'S ARGUABLY ONE OF THE BEST PLAYERS ever, a skater with electrifying quickness who could handle the puck deftly at break-neck speed. Pavel Bure was special in so many ways, from his patented dekes to his joyous celebrations after scoring goals for the Vancouver Canucks.

The Canucks learned right from his first game on November 5, 1991, that the 20-year-old Russian could become a game-breaking force, a player capable of not only scoring highlight-reel goals, but taking the team on a journey to the Stanley Cup Final by the spring of 1994.

But first, his Vancouver debut, a much anticipated event before a sold out Pacific Coliseum crowd of 16,123 that had heard all about the player called the Russian Rocket. Most had not seen the compact 185-pounder in person, just a few glimpses on television from the World Junior and World Championships when he played for the Soviet Union.

Vancouver management, led by Pat Quinn and Brian Burke, had astutely plucked Bure from under the noses of NHL rivals with a bold selection, 113th overall, in the 1989 entry draft. Most NHL teams didn't believe Bure was eligible, but the Canucks discovered Bure, then 18, had played the required 11 international games for his country, making him available for selection.

Another glorious moment for the Russian Rocket, celebrating a goal with Canucks teammates Jyrki Lumme (21) and Greg Adams.

"He sped into neutral ice at top speed, cut to his right and crossed the Winnipeg blueline, got around a Jets defenceman and fired a shot that was barely stopped."

Bure often stared pensively before a faceoff, but was always ready to explode ahead in search of scoring opportunities.

Two years later Bure arrived in Vancouver, well after the start of the regular season and having not played a competitive game in three months.

Canucks players, like their fans, didn't know what to expect, other than Bure was supposed to be a prospect who could make a difference.

"There was a buzz in the city about Pavel, but nobody really knew what he was capable of doing," recalls teammate Dave Babych. "He was kind of tentative in practice, although we soon learned he was quick and all that stuff. But it's hard to relate that to a game situation. We had to wait and see for ourselves."

Bure was pencilled in on the fourth line with Ryan Walter and Gino Odjick for his first NHL game against the Winnipeg Jets. Associate coach Rick Ley was in charge of the Canucks bench that night because Pat Quinn, the general manager and head coach, was attending league meetings in New York.

On his first shift, Bure went behind the Vancouver net and immediately showed what all the hype was about. He sped into neutral ice at top speed, cut to his right and crossed the Winnipeg blueline, got around a Jets defenceman and fired a shot that was barely stopped by netminder Rick Tabaracci. The Coliseum went from fans holding their breath in anticipation to an instantaneous outburst of appreciation, if not awe.

The Russian Rocket had landed.

"People got out of their seats and I'm sure they were thinking the same way the players were," says Babych. "Holy mackerel, he's pretty good. We hadn't seen speed like that for a long time. He handled the puck at top speed like an all star, like Guy Lafleur. He electrified the crowd.

Bure could lift an entire home crowd with his boyish enthusiasm after scoring one of his 254 goals with the Canucks.

It's the most significant goal in Canucks history as Pavel Bure slips a breakaway shot past Calgary goaltender Mike Vernon for the Game 7 overtime winner in 1994.

"A lot of guys can skate fast, but as soon as they get the puck they slow down a touch. Pavel made moves at top speed. His hands were as fast as his feet."

Bure didn't score that night, although he moved up to the second line after an injury to Jim Sandlak and was put into the clear in the third period by Cliff Ronning. The game ended in a 2-2 tie and a week later Bure got his first NHL goal on home ice against the Los Angeles Kings.

The Russian Rocket scored 34 times in 65 games during his first Canucks season, earning the Calder Trophy as the NHL's top rookie, and he would produce a team record 60-goal season the following campaign. The solidly built Bure, who bench pressed 200 pounds 14 times before stopping during an early workout with the Canucks, soon showed he could handle the rugged checking of the NHL.

Bure would go on to score 254 goals for Vancouver, plus another 34 in playoffs, but none was bigger than his overtime marker during the first round of the 1994 playoffs against the Calgary Flames. It was Game 7, second period of overtime in Calgary, when Bure scored a spectacular goal on a breakaway, giving the Canucks three consecutive overtime wins after trailing 3-1 in the series.

Defenceman Jeff Brown remembers the moment well because he was the one who made the immaculate breakaway pass to Bure following a cross-ice pass initiated by Babych.

"I remember making eye contact with Pavel," says Brown. "He knew I saw him and he found the seam between the two defencemen. Pavel did an amazing job of walking the line without going offside. He was just an incredible player and it was an unbelievable feeling when he jumped after scoring the goal."

Babych recalls the Canucks feeling invincible after beating Calgary and how the team went on to reach the Stanley Cup Final before losing in seven games to the New York Rangers.

"He had so much speed—speed to burn," Brown adds. "Pavel might have been the Alexander Ovechkin of the day. He could shoot, he was exciting, he could hit. He was just so dynamic."

Bure didn't finish his career with the Canucks, asking for a trade and later playing for the Florida Panthers and the Rangers. His career was cut short by a knee injury in the 2002-03 season, but not before he became legendary for his incredible ability to take over a game.

"I never saw another guy who got so jacked up over scoring a goal," says Canucks goalie Kirk McLean. "He just loved to score. He could easily win a game for you single-handedly—and often did."

GEOFF COURTNALL
Against all odds

GEOFF COURTNALL REMEMBERS VIVIDLY the almost eerie, silent flight to Calgary like it was yesterday, mostly because the Vancouver Canucks were on the verge of elimination from the 1994 NHL playoffs against their dreaded western rivals, the Calgary Flames.

The Canucks had won the first-round series opener by a convincing 5–0 margin in the Alberta foothills. Then came three straight stunning losses, including two at the Pacific Coliseum, and the Canucks were reeling. They needed an emotional lift.

They got it from Courtnall, a driven left winger who was a late bloomer in hockey terms, considering he didn't start playing the game until he was nine, after watching his three-year-old brother, Russ, begin to skate. Soccer was Geoff's game in the Vancouver Island community of Duncan, at least until he saw how much fun Russ was having on the ice.

Fast forward more than 20 years and Geoff was an accomplished NHL player, with his fifth NHL team, when he laced up his skates for the Canucks in the 1994 post-season. He had been acquired by the Canucks from the St. Louis Blues in a March 1991 trade that saw Vancouver acquire Courtnall, Cliff Ronning, Sergio Momesso and Robert Dirk in exchange for Garth Butcher and Dan Quinn.

Above: Courtnall had an eye for scoring important goals, none more significant than an overtime marker against the Calgary Flames in the 1994 playoffs.

Left: One of two Courtnall brothers to make it to the NHL, Geoff made the grade first, with Russ following in his footsteps. They later become teammates in Vancouver.

Courtnall didn't really want to leave St. Louis, where his teammates included Adam Oates, Brett Hull, Curtis Joseph and Rod Brind'Amour, but in his heart he had always wanted to play for Vancouver because the Canucks were considered

Geoff Courtnall pushes towards the net, trying to score on New York Rangers goalkeeper Mike Richter during the 1994 Stanley Cup Final.

his team while he was growing up, recalls the Victoria-born Courtnall.

Now, in late April 1994, Courtnall saw his Canucks teammates in dire need of a pick-me-up against the Flames, who had the venerable Mike Vernon in goal and a strong lineup that included Joe Nieuwendyk, Theo Fleury, Robert Reichel and Gary Roberts as top goal-scorers.

"I remember the flight to Calgary and everybody was pretty down about the way the series had turned against us," says Courtnall. "To be down 3–1 going back there against that team made it difficult.

"Once we got there, we had a quiet day. Everybody was pretty focussed on the game, knowing it was do-or-die. The game was really tight.

No one wanted to make a mistake at that point. Calgary kind of sat back and played disciplined defensively. They didn't want to open up against us."

The teams were tied 1–1 after three periods, forcing overtime. Kirk McLean was terrific in goal for the Canucks, as was Vernon for the Flames. It was the first sudden-death game of the series and tension mounted at the Saddledome, where Calgary fans anticipated their Flames moving into the second round of the playoffs.

"The game just seemed to go back and forth and there weren't a lot of scoring chances," Courtnall continues. "Then I was on a late change and got out of the box behind their defence. The puck just turned over and I got the chance we needed."

"You know, when you're from B.C., you always dream about playing for the Canucks. I got a chance to come home."

Nine goals in the 1994 playoff run highlighted a Courtnall career shortened by concussions.

Courtnall buried his shot behind Vernon at 7:15 of the first overtime period on April 26, 1994, and the Canucks lived to play another day.

He scored nine goals in the playoffs that year, none more significant than the one that began an amazing turnaround against Calgary which saw the Canucks win three consecutive games in overtime on markers by Courtnall, Trevor Linden and Pavel Bure.

Courtnall played on a forward line with centre Murray Craven and right winger Nathan LaFayette in the spring of 1994. The unit was probably considered the number-two or number-three attacking unit in Vancouver.

The top unit consisted of Linden between Greg Adams and Bure. Another line had Cliff Ronning pivoting Sergio Momesso and Martin Gelinas.

"Murray was great to play with because he was strong on faceoffs, very good defensively and a good passer, both forehand and backhand," says Courtnall. "He gave me some room to take some chances, and LaFayette had lots of speed he used to create chances."

In overtime situations, heroics sometimes come from sources other than top-line players, although Courtnall scored 367 goals during his 1,049-game NHL career, plus another 39 in 156 playoff games. He was a goal-scorer, for sure, an opportunist who made the most of his abilities.

He chuckles when recalling the moments leading up to his overtime marker in Calgary. He tells the story about how he and Ronning worked on their sticks in the hallway outside the Canucks dressing room. They sawed, whittled, heated, shaved and re-taped sticks, looking for just the right feel.

Courtnall was an emotional player who fed off his desire to succeed, even if it meant dropping his gloves from time to time.

Geoff will always be remembered by his fans in B.C., a fact he appreciates through his retirement years.

"Before the overtime, I told Cliffie I was putting a huge curve in my stick and if I get a chance, I'm going top shelf," Courtnall recalls. "I was heating up my stick and curving it in the hallway. Cliffie was laughing because the huge curve in my blade was probably illegal.

"I went top shelf, and we got to keep playing for a long time. It was just so exciting to win that Game 5. It was such a huge relief to win. It loosened everybody up. We really started to play well and come together after that."

Courtnall was thankful he had the opportunity to play with the Canucks during an NHL career that began as a free agent with the Boston Bruins in 1983. He had gone undrafted out of junior with the Victoria Cougars. He also would play for Edmonton and Washington before finishing with the Blues in 1999. He had two goals and four

points in six games with St. Louis that fall, but his career ended at age 37 due to concussions.

While with the Canucks, Courtnall got to play briefly with his brother Russ and was closer to his family ties on Vancouver Island.

"That goal in Calgary has stayed with me forever," Courtnall adds. "People still talk to me about it. You know, when you're from B.C., you always dream about playing for the Canucks. I got a chance to come home.

"In 1994 we had a team that came together at the right time. We did a lot of things as a group, like going paint-balling as a team. We had a lot of fun doing things like that. In the playoffs, we played for each other. That was the biggest thing."

Along with a little more curve on a stick blade that prolonged a season to remember.

GREG ADAMS
Timely scoring his trademark

THE SPORT OF HOCKEY has always been filled with great one-two combinations. Orr and Esposito. Bossy and Trottier. Gretzky and Kurri.

In the spring of 1994, in the east end of Vancouver, there emerged an unlikely duo: one man on the ice, the other in the broadcast booth.

"Linden into the Toronto zone, turning off the left boards . . . "

There's no way it was Jim Robson's best call during his three decades of sparkling play-by-play work for the Vancouver Canucks, but it was certainly memorable.

"Back at the line to Babych, long shot . . . "

As always, in his simple and brilliant style, Robson nailed the moment.

He had the ability to build to a crescendo without shouting. He had a voice that was down-home friendly, yet made you feel like you were listening to the most important event on the planet.

"Potvin had trouble with it . . . "

Now, there's a chance that, just before 11 p.m. on May 24, 1994, the most important event in the universe didn't take place at the Pacific Coliseum in Game 5 of the NHL's Western Conference final between the Canucks and Toronto Maple Leafs. Just don't tell that to a Canucks fan.

"Adams, shoots, scores!"

Greg Adams had been acquired by the Canucks from the New Jersey Devils seven years earlier, in a

Above: Adams had a knack for scoring overtime goals, which he did twice during the 1994 playoffs.

Left: The pride of Nelson, B.C., Greg Adams took on his father's nickname "Gus." In this case, it stood for "Goals Under Stress."

trade that saw Vancouver land another 1994 hero by the name of Kirk McLean. Adams's nickname was Gus, a tribute to his father. But during the Canucks' electric run through the '94 playoffs, Gus stood for G-U-S, as in "Goals Under Stress."

His knack for rippling the mesh at critical times during that post-season was extraordinary.

"I swear everyone on that team pitched in with a big goal at one time or another," says Adams. "I was fortunate enough to have a few of them."

"Greg Adams! Greg Adams!"

Adams (right) notched the overtime marker against Toronto that sent the Canucks to the '94 Stanley Cup Final, then raised the Clarence S. Campbell Bowl in celebration with teammates Sergio Momesso (left) and Trevor Linden.

It wasn't the first time Robson had used the Adams name in a hero's role.

Adams was the Vancouver player who scored late in the third period to force overtime in Game 7 of the Canucks' opening round matchup against Calgary. It was the goal that preceded *the* goal, Pavel Bure's breathtaking series winner, arguably the most memorable tally in Vancouver hockey history. Adams was also the player who went on to score the Canucks' overtime winner against the New York Rangers in Game 1 of the Stanley Cup Final. But, as momentous as that goal was, it didn't have the punch the May 24 marker did, if only because it didn't clinch a series.

"Adams gets the winner 14 seconds into the second overtime!"

It was, realistically, a game the Canucks shouldn't have won. They trailed the Leafs 3–0 after 20 minutes, but were able to roar back with three goals in the second period. Guess who scored the third goal to tie it up? That's right, the guy with the knack for rippling the mesh at critical times. Greg Adams, the lanky kid from Nelson, B.C., wearing Bobby Schmautz's old No. 8 jersey.

That game-tying goal was typical Adams: he converted a rebound while parked in front of the net where only the bravest of hockey players dare to venture. It's a dangerous, punishing area Adams never steered away from during a 17-year NHL career often interrupted by injuries. On this night, Adams' courage paid off not once, but twice: two goals against Felix Potvin, both from in close, one to tie the game, the other to win the series and move his team to the brink of NHL glory.

"The Vancouver Canucks are going to the Stanley Cup Final!"

Robson claims he was at a loss for words at that moment. "I've heard that call many times over," says the Hockey Hall of Famer. "I said Greg Adams' name three or four times. I couldn't think of anything else. I was excited!"

As for Adams, he was just happy his workday was done.

"Honestly, after all that hockey, I was so tired, my first reaction was, 'Finally, the game's over.' But then, I looked in the corner and saw the fans going crazy and that's when it all kicked in."

Adams retired from pro hockey in 2003 to live year-round in Phoenix, something avid Canadian golfers have a tendency to do. And every now and then, he'll throw in a DVD or log on to YouTube to reminisce.

"It wasn't the prettiest goal," admits Adams. "Jim made it sound much better than it was."

Adams and Robson. They'll be forever linked in Canucks history: Adams for scoring one of the franchise's most significant goals; Robson for describing it in perfect fashion.

Adams scored 65 power play goals during his Canucks career and a total of 179 goals.

MARKUS NASLUND

A 12-year love affair with Vancouver

Above: Canucks captain Naslund was a tried and true professional who took his position seriously.

Left: A model of consistency, Naslund carried himself with pride and dignity, both on and off the ice.

"All I can say is every game I played, I was proud to wear a Canucks' jersey. I will always remember those 12 years fondly. It's a hard thing to leave. I always envisioned myself retiring as a Canuck."

—Markus Naslund, July 3, 2008, the day he signed with the New York Rangers

HE NEVER GOT THE CHANCE TO SAY GOODBYE. After more goals (346) and points (756) than any Canuck in history—more than Stan Smyl, more than Trevor Linden—Markus Naslund left the franchise as a notation on the NHL's transaction wire three days into free agency in the summer of 2008.

He was at his summer home in Sweden at the time, with his wife Lotta and the three children who were born in Vancouver and considered it home.

None of them were able to say goodbye.

So the following May, after Naslund's season with the New York Rangers was over and before the winger announced he was retiring at age 36 from the NHL (despite having one year and $4-million remaining on his contract), the greatest scorer in Canuck history quietly slipped back into Vancouver for four days so his family, and especially his kids, could gain some closure.

"It was for the kids as much as for us," Naslund said a year later.

Naslund eyes the puck and heads towards the net for another scoring chance, this one against Dallas Drake and the St. Louis Blues.

"They never had the chance to say bye to their friends when we changed cities. So they went back to their school and had a chance to meet with their friends and see them. Mostly, we tried to make it so the kids had their say and they could choose to do whatever they wanted."

But while Rebecca, Isabella and Alex got to see their friends from the old neighbourhood in Point Grey and eat at their favourite restaurants and do their favourite things, the homecoming was also a powerful experience for Naslund.

He said everything evoked memories for him. He said he couldn't drive over the Lions Gate Bridge without remembering bringing his newborn children home from the hospital. He remembered taking little Rebecca up the Grouse Grind, biking with friends, taking the kids to the beach at English Bay, and walking on forest trails near the University of British Columbia.

"Those memories are part of my life and always will be," he said.

Mostly, he remembers what it was like to be a Canuck, to captain the team for seven seasons, and be at the epicentre of the franchise's intense, crazy relationship with its fans and experiencing all the good and bad that this entailed.

Markus Naslund was the reliable centre-piece of the Canucks offence for many years, especially when flanked by Todd Bertuzzi (left) and Brendan Morrison (right).

Towards the end of his 12 years, Naslund seemed at times to love Vancouver more than it loved him back. Some fans found it inexcusable that Naslund should age, that he would erode in the least from the dominant scorer who set a Canucks record (that may never be broken) when he was named to the NHL's First All-Star Team three successive years starting in 2002.

In 2003, when he established career highs with 48 goals and 104 points, Naslund became the first Canuck to win the Lester B. Pearson Award, bestowed to the NHL's best player, by its players.

Naslund finished his career with respectable seasons of 24 goals, 25 goals and 24 goals. Yet, on April 5, 2008, the last of his 884 games as a Canuck, against the Calgary Flames, was lost in the emotional vortex created by Trevor Linden's final game.

Linden has said he regrets that his last game shrouded Naslund's final night as a Canuck.

"I have no hard feelings at all," Naslund said. "I thought it was great to see Trevor get the appreciation he deserved. Everyone kind of knew it was Trevor's last game. For me, it wasn't my last game. But it was my last game in Vancouver."

Naslund said he is proud that he was part of the Canucks franchise's rebirth at the start of this century, that he helped fill a building that had been half-empty in the late 1990s, and captained a team that eclipsed 100 points three times and went to the Stanley Cup playoffs five times in six seasons.

His greatest regret? The same as everyone else's.

"To this day, if we'd had the right timing I think we could have gone real far in the playoffs," Naslund said. "I thought strongly we had a chance of winning a Stanley Cup. But it never happened.

"There is such a fine line between having success and not having success.

"Sometimes it's out of your control. You think: Could I have put in more effort, could I have done something different? But at some point, you just have to let it go."

Then, all that's left are the happy memories.

MARC CRAWFORD

"Crow" flew in opposite directions in summer and winter

THE BUDDY SYSTEM NEVER worked for Marc Crawford. He was emotional and darn proud of it during his tenure behind the bench of the Vancouver Canucks.

The head coach, nicknamed "Crow," would call out his players in public, pick at them in private, and even had a few choice words for NHL officials and beat writers, too. Can't take it? Too bad.

Crawford was "Summer" Crow and "Winter" Crow. He was relaxed in summer and outwardly critical in hockey season. He learned over the years to temper his outbursts.

"Getting mad is not going to help anybody," says Crawford. "You've got to be a teacher and be logical and step away for half a second. It's changed because of the salary cap. Trades don't happen. You've got to work through issues and give it a second, third or fourth try. You can't cast away problems and hide your issues by buying another piece. That doesn't happen anymore.

"But you do have to be yourself. I'm not going to change. I'm always going to be an emotional coach and always be a guy who is passionate. But you temper it."

As much as Crawford has adapted, he's not that far removed from the hard-headed mentor who compiled a franchise record 246 career wins in seven seasons behind the Vancouver bench, after replacing the fired Mike Keenan in January

Above: Emotional and passionate, Crawford can't see himself changing his coaching style despite his critics.

Left: Called the "Crow" by hockey insiders, Marc Crawford pauses to listen to a young Henrik Sedin (33) on the Canucks bench, while Daniel Sedin eavesdrops.

Summit meetings like this rarely end in the head coach's favour. Crawford learned the men in stripes usually get their way.

1999. Those victories often came from the artistry of the West Coast Express trio of Markus Naslund, Brendan Morrison and Todd Bertuzzi. However, those run-and-gun Canucks won just one playoff round during Crawford's tenure and when the club collapsed to miss the post-season in 2005–06, it cost the Belleville, Ontario, native his job.

But not his belief in what could have been.

The best title for the franchise chapter under Crawford guidance might be "Great Expectations."

"When I think of it, it's what a great run we had," recalls Crawford.

"When we won the division [in 2003–04] it was huge, but my biggest disappointment was the Minnesota series [in 2002–03]. I think: 'God,

I should have been able to do something different.' I should have been able to nurse the team because I thought it unfolded for us. That's the one that keeps you awake at night."

The road to the Stanley Cup seemed paved with potential in the spring of 2003, with second-seed Detroit and third-seed Colorado losing in the first round. When the Canucks rallied from a 3–1 series deficit against St. Louis, there was obvious optimism. They then built a 3–1 second-round stranglehold on Minnesota, but stumbled on their mission to make short work of the Wild. And even though the Canucks were back in the post-season mix the following spring, an overtime loss to Calgary in the seventh game of that opening-round

Crawford is vocal in game situations and his attention to detail resulted in 246 regular season wins, most ever by a Canucks coach.

series only brought the Minnesota disappointment back into focus.

However, a high-tempo, we-can-outscore-you approach made Crawford's clubs entertaining and dangerous.

And, keeping the West Coast Express from derailing was a challenge because of the three distinct personalities that comprised the NHL's best line. When Crawford resorted to his Winter Crow persona and pecked away at his stars, it was Morrison who often suffered the bruised ego. But it was done with purpose. The centre could handle the heat, knowing his coach could motivate the masses through him.

"It wasn't quite that simple," says Crawford. "Mo is one of the smartest who ever played for me and I really appreciated him. When you give him something to absorb, it doesn't get caught in the noise of the message. That's a unique ability. And let's face it. I can be noisy."

Bertuzzi was once the game's premier power forward and clashed with Crawford in much the same manner as he would barge his way to the net. Imposing on the ice, he was also a brooding presence off it. He had a lukewarm relationship with the media, and with Crawford too.

"In the end, we probably co-existed," Crawford says of Bertuzzi. "It soured when he wanted to be more of a finesse player and we needed him to be the power player. The give-and-take with Todd was always about me trying to get him to be more forceful."

A high-tempo, we-can-outscore-you approach made Crawford's clubs entertaining and dangerous.

Crawford also saw Naslund's numbers tail off and the forces at play to make the captain as accountable on the ice as off it were immense. The glare of the media spotlight was intense. So was the demand of the coach to get the most out of his best player. At one point, Naslund was the game's premier left winger, but it was as if there was an expiry date on the Swede—just like Crawford. Yet, in the end, Crawford has nothing but admiration for what Naslund accomplished and endured.

"His character was unquestionable. He was outstanding, a great captain who did the best he could and is one of the top players in Canucks history."

Crawford also forged a history with Hockey Canada and is best remembered for his shootout strategy in the 1998 Winter Olympics at Nagano, Japan.

Needing a goal from Trevor Linden with 67 seconds remaining to extend a semi-final clash with the Czech Republic, Team Canada couldn't get to red-hot goaltender Dominik Hasek in 10 minutes of overtime and dropped a bitter 2–1 shootout decision.

As head coach, Crawford reasoned that Theoren Fleury, Ray Bourque, Joe Nieuwendyk, Eric Lindros and Brendan Shanahan were his best bets in the five-player skills competition to beat Hasek. None of them could, and Robert Reichel was the lone Czech shooter to solve Patrick Roy. When the TV camera panned to a disconsolate Wayne Gretzky sitting alone on the bench long after the final outcome, the debate raged. How could the Great One not be included in the shootout—especially with the injured Joe Sakic and Paul Kariya unavailable?

"I made the decision based on what I thought was going to give us the best chance to win,' recalls Crawford. "There's no other rationale than that. I sometimes wonder if I should have changed it, but it was a different era. We're all used to the shootout now and everybody accepts it. We were absolutely terrified of it and the Czechs played to get to it because they weren't terrified."

In retrospect, Crawford says that Eric Lindros may not have been the right captain for that team. And putting too much emphasis on checking and not enough on speed also hurt Team Canada.

"We should have made Gretzky the captain," admits Crawford. "And it was a huge mistake to not bring Scott Niedermayer in and not realizing how important skating is in the Olympics. And at that time, the prevailing thought was you needed a line of true checkers and that's why [Rob] Zamuner and [Keith] Primeau and [Rod] Brind'Amour were brought in. You need top players who have the ability to check."

Through it all Crawford grew to become a better coach. He learned to stop baiting referees. He learned to stop being slapped with fines, and even ejected from a game in St. Louis in March 2003 for arguing penalties. And he learned to call out his players in private, not in public.

"I knew better," chuckles Crawford. "You slip up, but I didn't slip a lot."

There are many times when a coach has little left but to coax his players into listening. Crawford puts that theory to work here.

"Crow" on his perch behind the Canucks bench led the team into the playoffs four straight years, beginning in the spring of 2001.

HENRIK AND DANIEL SEDIN
Burke drew two aces

THE NHL ENTRY DRAFT has often been described as a "crapshoot" and the Canucks have had their share of risky and uncertain ventures over the years, right from the beginning when they lost the number-one pick on the spin of a roulette wheel. Vancouver's first-ever choice in 1970 was defenceman Dale Tallon, while their expansion cousins, the Buffalo Sabres, got to pick future Hall of Famer Gilbert Perreault.

The NHL reinforces the idea that the entry draft is a gamble by holding a lottery, complete with numbered bingo balls, to determine the selection order for non-playoff teams. The Canucks have won some and lost some on draft day, but rarely have they held the spotlight as they did June 26, 1999, in Boston, when general manager Brian Burke went "all in" and turned up a full house, with two aces, Daniel and Henrik Sedin.

"There was no gamble when it came to the players," says Mike Penny, who was the Canucks' director of scouting that year. "Our scout in Europe, Thomas Gradin, had them on his radar screen way before they were draft eligible. By the time the draft rolled around, it was no big secret that they were the best players on the board. They were ranked 1–2 in Europe and they were co-MVPs in the Swedish Elite League."

"It was one of those rare times when everyone in the hockey department was in complete

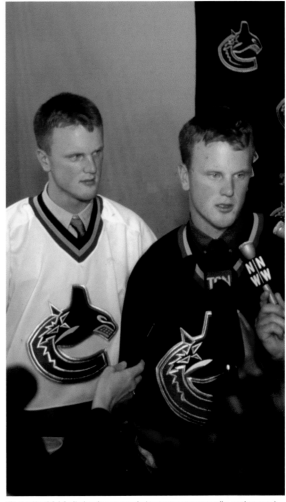

Above: Youthful Sedin brothers wear their new sweaters proudly, as they speak to the Vancouver media.

Left: A hug, a smile and a victory salute: a scene that would become familiar to Canucks fans after the arrival of the identical twins from Sweden.

agreement on the players," says Steve Tambellini, the team's director of player personnel at the time. "Brian [Burke] did a great job to make it happen. I'm not sure you could do something like that today, the way the contracts are. It was unique, no doubt about it."

The Canucks had to make no less than three deals, with Chicago, Tampa Bay and Atlanta, so they could manoeuvre into position to control the draft with the second and third picks overall.

Burke's first approach was to the Blackhawks. "Their GM, Bob Murray, knew exactly what we were trying to do," recalls Burke. "We wound up doing a handshake deal the Sunday before the draft. It was an expensive deal. We gave up defenceman Bryan McCabe and a couple of first-round picks, but we knew these kids were going to be something special."

Burke played his hand with amazing aplomb in working the draft to fully benefit the Canucks.

The Sedins were hoping they would not be separated by the draft, but knew anything was possible with so many teams in play. Tampa Bay held the first pick and general manager Rick Dudley was determined to draft Daniel Sedin.

This is where Burke played some hardball with Dudley and hit a home run.

"Dudley was tough as a player and he was tough to make deals with as a GM," says Burke. "But the conversation changed once he realized that we had Chicago's pick and control of the draft. I told him that we would draft Henrik and then we could both go to the media and announce that we'd drafted a player that we couldn't bring in because they wouldn't come unless they came together. About an hour before the draft, we made the deal."

Once the Canucks had the first overall pick, it was an easy sell for Burke to move it to expansion Atlanta in exchange for the number-two choice and complete the most dramatic draft day in team history.

"I didn't want to draft them separately," says Burke. "The money shot that day had to be the twins, on stage, together."

Henrik is six minutes older than Daniel, they are separated by one inch in height (Henrik is

taller), and by one position to the left on the forward line (Henrik is the centre). Their uniform numbers, 22 and 33, reflect their draft positions in 1999, second (Daniel) and third (Henrik).

A decade later, the identical twins from Örnsköldsvik, Sweden, were still the "money shot," on stage, together.

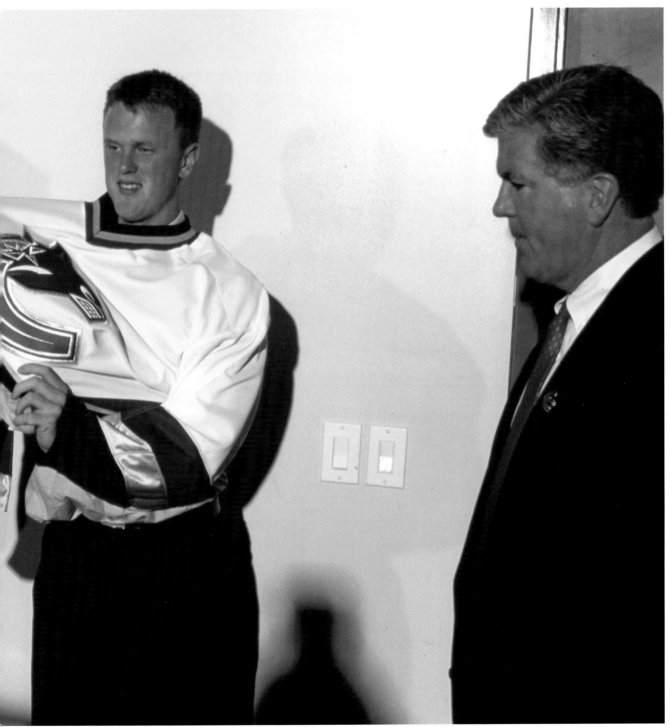

At first, even general manager Brian Burke, who drafted the Sedins, couldn't figure out which was which, or who was who.

"I didn't want to draft them separately," says Burke. "The money shot that day had to be the twins, on stage, together."

WEST COAST EXPRESS
High-voltage offence

IT WAS THE NHL'S BEST AND MOST EXCITING forward line. It provided destination viewing for fans across North America and rekindled interest in a team that had missed the playoffs four of the previous five seasons. It was dubbed "The West Coast Express" as the most entertaining and productive trio the Canucks had ever known, and it came together thanks to Trent Klatt.

Not that it was his idea, but Klatt was the key player who allowed coach Marc Crawford to put Markus Naslund, Todd Bertuzzi and Brendan Morrison together during the 2001–02 season.

It was the line that defined the Canucks for the next three years.

"We all had a hunger and desire to perform at our best each night," says Morrison. "We were extremely competitive and we pushed each other to become better players."

Naslund considers those West Coast years some of the happiest of his professional career, a time when he was comfortable with the situation because the trio got along so well.

"All three of us had different personalities," Naslund recalls. "We had a lot of fun, on and off the ice, when we were together. That's part of why we had success. We liked being around each other. There's definitely a lot of fond memories when I look back."

At the season's outset, Naslund was a 27-year-old team captain fresh off a breakthrough

Above: Brendan Morrison played a pivotal role in keeping his line productive as he set up plays for his high-profile wingers.

Left: Markus Naslund (19) stands at attention for the national anthem alongside linemate and close friend Todd Bertuzzi.

Fans were treated to end-to-end rushes, spectacular goals and an offence that continually pressed ahead, often at breakneck speed.

The West Coast Express, flanked by defencemen Scott LaChance (14) and Ed Jovanovski (55).

campaign when he'd scored 41 goals playing mostly with centre Andrew Cassels.

Bertuzzi, at 25 and with six years in the league, was becoming a strong power forward and had scored 25 goals the season before.

Morrison, 26, had come in a deadline deal a year earlier and was a durable playmaker who lived on the second or third line with Matt Cooke.

Morrison killed penalties and could also play the point on the power play.

Bertuzzi played on occasion with Naslund and Cassels, especially on the power play, but he was needed elsewhere because there was a piece of the puzzle missing.

The Sedin twins, Daniel and Henrik, were 21 and in their second NHL season. They were clearly great together, but Crawford had trouble finding a right winger who could complement their cycle game, stay out of their way and yet still cash in on their superb playmaking. Most games, Crawford felt that's where he needed Bertuzzi.

Enter Klatt, a 30-year-old veteran checker who was a good team man and penalty-killer, but was seldom counted on to score goals.

Morrison is mobbed by teammates Ed Jovanovski (55), Markus Naslund (19), Todd Bertuzzi (44) and Matt Cooke (24) following a power-play goal against Edmonton.

One early November night in Columbus, with Cassels unable to play because of an injury, Crawford—a constant line juggler—started the game with Morrison as his number-one centre playing with Naslund and Klatt.

Bertuzzi was with the twins. On an early power play, Bertuzzi took Klatt's place and, for one of the first times, Naslund, Morrison and Bertuzzi were together on a forward line.

Despite a good night in a 3–2 win, the launch of the Express was aborted. Cassels returned and Klatt got hurt, so Bertuzzi was back with the twins and Morrison was bumped back a notch or two.

On January 23, 2002, the lineup was healthy again and the time was right for another switch.

Crawford hadn't forgotten how well Klatt worked with the twins.

Bertuzzi, Naslund and Morrison went together and scored five points collectively in a 4–2 win in Dallas and that was it. They were together for the next three-and-a-half seasons.

"We each brought something different to the line," Morrison analyzes.

"Markus was the pure goal scorer with underrated passing skills. Todd was the premier power forward at the time with his physicality and finesse, and I brought speed and playmaking."

Crawford liked his two top scorers, "Nazzy and Bert," together. He'd been impressed at how well Morrison worked with them on the power play

Naslund takes the traditional route in celebrating another goal by the popular West Coast Express.

Naslund, Bertuzzi and Henrik Sedin share some encouraging words after scoring.

and, moreover, felt Morrison could handle the demands of playing with two guys who always wanted the puck, let him hear about it when they didn't get it and were angry if they didn't score.

But score they did as the West Coast Express was on track and fans were treated to end-to-end rushes, spectacular goals and an offence that continually pressed ahead, often at breakneck speed.

"We had a great response from the Vancouver fans and it was important because it came at a time when there was a bit of a transition for the Canucks," recalls Naslund. "We came together at the right time and the team became much more competitive. It seemed the three of us matured all at the same time. I'll never forget those years with the Canucks."

The following season, the line was nothing short of magnificent. Led by Naslund and his 48 goals and 104 points, the trio scored 119 goals and 272 points. Naslund and Bertuzzi were both first team all stars and Naslund won the Pearson Trophy for the most outstanding player, as voted by the NHL Players' Association. The wingers finished second and fifth in league scoring. On the power play they were almost unstoppable.

Bertuzzi, with his patented push-off move, scored 25 and Naslund, with an incomparable wrist shot, had 24 power play goals that season, far and away the best power-play totals in the league.

For his part, Morrison was the glue that held the line together. He took the directions Crawford issued for the line and much of the heat when they weren't productive—which wasn't very often.

"It was a tremendous time in my career," concedes Morrison. "As an offensive player it was an amazing feeling knowing that our line could score any time we were on the ice."

At the time the NHL was desperately seeking goals. Stifling defensive schemes had slowed games to a standstill, but the Canucks had their big line. With Ed Jovanovski on the back end, they were a breath of fresh air and like rock stars around the league.

For the first time in the team's history, crowds gathered around the Canucks' bus on the road and thousands of fans wore Vancouver sweaters in buildings everywhere. They were the NHL's great late-night movie, an attacking team among the mad trappers, with "The West Coast Express" in the starring role.

ROYALTY
Queen Elizabeth II gets red carpet welcome

Above: Her Majesty Queen Elizabeth was flanked by Wayne Gretzky and British Columbia Premier Gordon Campbell in the Royal Box. The esteemed guest of the Canucks showed a keen interest in what was happening below at ice level.

Left: Hockey Hall of Fame member Wayne Gretzky was all smiles when Queen Elizabeth II dropped the puck at GM Place on October 6, 2002. Markus Naslund (19), captain of the Canucks, faced off with Mike Ricci of the San Jose Sharks in the red carpet occasion. Canadian Olympian Cassie Campbell was part of the procession, along with Ed Jovanovski of the Canucks. They were gold medallists at the 2002 Olympics.

IT WAS A FLASHPOINT FOR ROYALTY WATCHERS when ruling monarch Queen Elizabeth II walked along the red carpet placed over freshly flooded ice at General Motors Place in the fall of 2002.

The queen was there for a ceremonial faceoff before an NHL pre-season game on October 6 involving the Vancouver Canucks and the San Jose Sharks that drew far more attention than most games that time of year.

She was in Vancouver during her hectic Golden Jubilee Tour of Canada to honour Canadian Olympians Ed Jovanovski of the Canucks and Cassie Campbell, captain of the Canadian women's team, for their gold medal performances that year at the Salt Lake City Winter Olympics.

Her Majesty was in rare form for the curious faceoff between Canucks captain Markus Naslund and San Jose centre Mike Ricci, whose shoulder-length hair was tucked under his helmet and into his sweater for the occasion.

Referee Rob Shick recalls being instructed by protocol officials to take the puck, which had a

Canucks captain Markus Naslund, pictured on the overhead video screen, spoke briefly with Queen Elizabeth following the ceremonial puck drop, while both teams and invited minor hockey players enjoyed the vista.

The queen must have enjoyed the hockey because, before leaving midway through the game, she asked both Gretzky and Meeker what channel it would be on at her hotel.

Vancouver Canucks logo, to the queen and be at her side without being intrusive.

After the puck dropped, Naslund naturally handed it back to the queen. Shick says she had noticed the logo and suddenly asked Naslund if he wanted to keep the puck.

"No," Naslund replied. "We've got lots, thanks."

At least that's how Shick remembers the brief conversation between HRH Queen Elizabeth and the Canucks' respectful captain.

The on-ice procession for the faceoff also included British Columbia Premier Gordon Campbell, hockey legend Howie Meeker from the Vancouver Island community of Parksville and Canadian hockey icon Wayne Gretzky, who had been executive director of the 2002 Canadian men's Olympic team that beat the United States 5–2 in the gold medal game at Salt Lake.

Meeker lauded the puck-dropping style of the queen, noting it was much better than that of some NHL linesmen. Gretzky was seated next to the queen in the temporary Royal Box during the first period and recalled her "letting us know when people were getting hit. She was curious about the penalties and impressed with how fast the goaltenders were."

Gretzky told reporters that the queen did wonderfully with the puck drop. "Her technique was just fine," he said. "She did a tremendous job."

It was important for Canada to show the queen the game the country loves with such passion, Gretzky later said, and the significance of winning the gold medal. He also noted how pleased

the queen was when Jovanovski scored the first goal in the pre-season game. He had been wearing street clothes and his No. 55 Canucks jersey for the pre-game ceremonies and had to change quickly before coming into the game.

"Him getting the first goal, that really perked her up," Gretzky said.

The Canucks won 3–2 that night, although Ricci scored both San Jose goals and joked that maybe the queen should fly in for all his games.

It was the third time the queen had participated in a ceremonial faceoff in Canada, having been the guest for pre-game ceremonies in Montreal and Toronto in 1951 when she was a princess.

For the excitable Meeker, it was the second time he'd been on the ice with Her Majesty. He had been with the Toronto Maple Leafs 51 years earlier when she dropped the puck before a game against the Chicago Blackhawks.

Meeker remembers that he was standing beside Toronto captain Teeder Kennedy when Leafs owner Conn Smythe brought the princess over to meet Kennedy.

"That picture, with Teeder bowing to the princess, was on the front of our next program," says Meeker.

Fast-forward 51 years and Meeker is at GM Place, talking with Prince Philip, the Duke of Edinburgh, in the Royal Box during the first period. Meeker had a photograph from the Toronto ceremony and wanted it autographed.

"I showed the picture to him and asked if the queen would like to see it," Meeker says. "She did, gave it a look and said, 'I remember that. I still have

Canada's national anthem was never more meaningful than the night Her Majesty stood alongside Wayne Gretzky at centre ice with Canadian Olympic gold medallists Ed Jovanovski of the Canucks and Cassie Campbell to their right and Howie Meeker to their left.

the puck they gave me.' Well, we talked a little longer and the queen went back to watching the game with Gretzky and Premier Campbell. Then I asked the duke if he'd like to sign the picture. He looked down and grunted something. He didn't sign it, so I put it away. Still, it was a wonderful experience.

"That was quite a walk out there on the red carpet with the queen in front of us. The place really warmed up to her. They say the queen's popularity has dropped. Absolutely not, I say."

Shick remembers anxious moments he had before the game when he was waiting off to the side before the procession went on ice.

"Wayne Gretzky was standing there, so I asked him if he remembered the outdoor exhibition game we did in Las Vegas many years before," recalled Shick. "He just looked at me and laughed because he thought he'd seen it all, and now we were about to be on the ice with the queen.

"When I got on the ice, there was no warm-up lap to get my feet feeling right in my skates. So I just went from the tunnel to the referee's crease by the timekeeper's box. My biggest fear was catching an edge. I took the easy way out and stepped on the carpet about 15 feet early and walked over

to the queen, careful to be at her side and not in front.

"I think she was taken aback a bit by the ambience and everything. I know the teams didn't want to fight at all with the queen in the building. I think we had a no-hitter that night."

Shick didn't get to speak directly with the queen, but he was given a keepsake, a photo of himself with the queen and Gretzky, with Jovanovski and Cassie Campbell in the background. Shick had the photograph enlarged and presented it to the city of Port Alberni, where it hangs in his hometown arena.

The queen must have enjoyed the hockey because, before leaving midway through the game, she asked both Gretzky and Meeker what channel it would be on at her hotel.

It was on Canucks TV because the game was produced by the team for a pay-for-view audience.

For history buffs, the Canucks won 3–2 that night, with the other two goals scored by rookie Fedor Fedorov, who would not score in seven Vancouver games during the regular season.

He, like Ricci, did some of his best work when watched by royalty.

CANUCKS OWNERSHIP
Long-time Vancouver family seeks the Stanley Cup

FRANCESCO AQUILINI TELLS THE STORY about being a young boy growing up in the east end of Vancouver when he would wait outside the Pacific Coliseum hoping to catch a glimpse of his hockey heroes. His fondest memory was meeting Swedish defenceman Lars Lindgren, who gave him a souvenir hockey stick.

It was a big-league thrill for a kid now at the helm of the organization he has always adored. Francesco and his brothers, Roberto and Paolo, are managing partners in the Aquilini Investment Group of Vancouver that owns 100 per cent of Canucks Sports & Entertainment. While the day-to-day operations remain in the hands of the Aquilini brothers, their father, Luigi, continues to play an active role in mentoring the organization he created. "The way it works," Francesco explains, "with my brothers and Dad and me, everything is a collaborative effort. And I mean everything."

Following in the footsteps of former owners Thomas Scallen, Frank Griffiths, Arthur Griffiths and John McCaw, Jr., the Aquilinis became the fifth owners of the team in 2004. But it was more than just a business transaction to the family. It was a commitment that the best was yet to come in Vancouver.

The Canucks, back in local hands exclusively for the first time since the Griffiths family were sole owners of the team, have blossomed under

Above: Flanked by brothers Roberto (left) and Paolo (right), Canucks chairman and NHL governor Francesco Aquilini acts as family liaison with management on a daily basis.

Left: A proud Francesco Aquilini shares at his inaugural press conference that he and his family are driven to bring an NHL playoff championship to Vancouver.

the Aquilini regime, topping 100 points, winning the Northwest Division and making it to the Western Conference semi-finals in three of the last four seasons.

Impressive, yet those feats don't measure up to the Aquilinis' most important accomplishment: they've changed the culture of the team and made the Canucks one of the most desired clubs to play

The Aquilini Investment Group is introduced as an official supplier for the 2010 Olympics by organizing committee CEO John Furlong (second from left) and mascots (left to right) Sumi, Miga and Quatchi.

for in the National Hockey League. No corners have been cut in upgrading the team and arena, including spending almost $40 million in improvements such as a lavish world class dressing room, innovative player development and scouting initiatives, a state of the art, high definition score clock and broadcast facilities. The Aquilinis also spearheaded a strategic alliance with Rogers Communications Inc., giving Rogers the arena-naming and telecommunications sponsorship rights to the home of the Vancouver Canucks, the newly renamed Rogers Arena. Pair all that with Vancouver's standing as one of the greatest cities in the world, and it's no wonder the franchise is home to some of the biggest superstars in hockey and the most passionate fans in the league.

It all starts with the right attitude, and from day one the Aquilinis have had it. "We are driven to bring the Stanley Cup to our community and reach out to every hockey fan across the entire province," Francesco proclaimed at the family's inaugural press conference upon taking over ownership.

Pride in their craft has been a hallmark of the Aquilini family since Luigi founded the Aquilini Investment Group, one of British Columbia's most diversified local enterprises, more than 50 years ago. The firm is a leader in commercial development and construction and has a broad national real estate portfolio that includes commercial properties, office buildings, hotels, golf courses, restaurants, and cranberry and blueberry farms.

That local touch has translated into a greater sense of community pride and responsibility for the franchise.

The annual family skating party at Christmas is always popular with members of the Canucks organization as Paolo Aquilini guides youngster Mason Lee around the ice.

Not since the Griffiths, who owned the team from 1974 to 1997, has a family with roots entangled so deeply in Vancouver overseen the Canucks. That local touch has translated into a greater sense of community pride and responsibility for the franchise.

Along with the Aquilini family's ongoing community support, they have continued the franchise's tradition of being the backbone of numerous charitable endeavours through unwavering support for the Canucks for Kids Fund, the team's signature charity that bolsters regional charities to the tune of $3 million a year, the recently launched Canucks Autism Network, as well as the active support of Canuck Place Children's Hospice.

With such a mountain of responsibility, you'd expect Francesco Aquilini's head to be spinning, but working as family liaison with the Canucks' management hardly feels like a job. The 10-year-old Francesco is long gone, but the desire he had then for Vancouver to be on top of the hockey world remains steadfast today. The hockey stick he got from Lindgren has served as a reminder of his end goal and a recent encounter with his one-time hero demonstrated just how far he's come.

Roughly 37 years after meeting one of his biggest Canucks idols, Aquilini was in Las Vegas at the invitation of general manager Mike Gillis, who was holding meetings with his entire scouting staff, which included Lindgren.

Aquilini and Lindgren met once again, only this time the admiration and respect was mutual.

ROBERTO LUONGO
"Bobby Loooo" commits playoff larceny

MENTION APRIL 11, 2007, to Roberto Luongo and he'll instantly know why it's significant. Like the day he got married, or the day he became a father, some dates will never be erased from the memory bank.

It wasn't just the first career playoff test for the Vancouver Canucks goaltender, who was already under the probing National Hockey League microscope of great expectations. It was a game that started on a Wednesday evening and ended early Thursday. And when Henrik Sedin finally ended the extended drama by swatting a pass from brother Daniel past Marty Turco at 78 minutes, six

Above: Luongo's legendary larceny comes into play when he stares down opposing shooters. His concentration is evident game after game.

Left: Striking an intimidating pose, Roberto Luongo has been the guardian of the Canucks' net worth. His gold medal performance at the 2010 Olympic Winter Games only solidified his status as the fans' favourite.

seconds of overtime, Luongo knew the franchise's longest game—the sixth longest in league history—was special.

It didn't measure up in duration to the league record 116:30 the Detroit Red Wings needed on March 24, 1936, to edge the Montreal Maroons 1-0, but Luongo's performance was measured in more than minutes.

Luongo made 72 saves. He remembers some. He can't remember others because of the fatigue brought on by the frenetic pace—the Canucks had been outshot 16-3 in the third period alone. And when the issue was finally settled, the Canucks were outshot 76-53 in the stunning 5-4 victory over the Dallas Stars that was Luongo's biggest effort of that season.

It might have been the biggest game of his career, because it set the tone for the tough series.

"What I remember after the game was over was just going and lying down on the trainer's table for about 30 minutes and not moving," Luongo recalls with a chuckle. "It was definitely weird; nobody thought the game would go that long.

"It's funny. As a kid growing up, I watched a lot of playoff hockey and when they got to four or five overtimes I wondered: 'How do they do that? How do they go so long without allowing a goal?' And just being a part of that, it's crazy. You get into a mindset. After the second or third overtime,

It's always a good sign when Roberto Luongo raises his arms in celebration because that means the Canucks have won another game at home.

He compiled a .931 save percentage— first among stoppers with more than 50 starts—and had seven shutouts.

A bird's-eye view from inside the net: Luongo flashes his glove hand to stymie Chicago Blackhawks' Captain Jonathan Toews.

you're so tired. Fatigue is really a factor and you just try to be as focussed as you can and do whatever you can to get in front of the puck."

While Luongo would go on to backstop the Canucks to a seven-game, nail-biting series victory, his first career post-season triumph put in perspective his steady rise from prospect to prime-time player. He wasn't at his best that April night. Pucks were popping out of his glove, his positioning wasn't sharp and he was serving up rebounds with alarming regularity.

With the Canucks leading 4-2 in the third period, the Stars struck twice in a six-minute span to tie the score and set the stage for a dramatic finish.

In the first overtime, Luongo made a tough pad save off Loui Eriksson.

In the second overtime, he stopped a shot by Jere Lehtinen and then Nagy on the ensuing

rebound. That was followed by a spectacular glove save off Mattias Norstrom after the defenceman stepped around Ryan Kesler and whipped a shot destined for the top corner. Then came another glove save off Stu Barnes.

"Oh, yeah. I remember most of the goals," adds Luongo. "I can't tell you that I remember all of them, but I remember some plays that stand out.

"There was a wrap-around in overtime and I was so tired, I just had my legs against the post because that's all I could do. Somehow the puck didn't go in.

"I can't remember all the intermissions, but there were definitely a lot of oranges and making sure you get as many fluids as you can, because by that point you're pretty depleted."

Luongo managed to adapt to the hockey-mad Vancouver market after the Florida Panthers

Luongo doesn't stand alone at his end of the rink: he has plenty of support from the White Towel Brigade during home games.

traded him to the Canucks on June 23, 2006. Canuck fans took to him immediately and chanted "Loooo, Loooo" after his many great saves.

Earlier in his career, Luongo often struggled under the glare of the media spotlight. However, buoyed by advice from former team captain Trevor Linden—he urged the goalie to remember that if you resist, they [the media] will persist—a summer of transition in 2008 saw Luongo evolve from evasive to engaging. And when he was offered the captaincy that fall, the pieces effortlessly fell into place. He wanted to lead on and off the ice. Now he had the talent and the confidence to do both.

"It was a great honour when it happened and a great surprise," he recalls. "Just the fact I'm the only goalie [in the league] who's a captain, I take a lot of pride in that. I try to do the best job I can. Lead by example and work as hard as I can in practice and games and you also want to have a good relationship with the media. You don't want it [captaincy] to weigh on your shoulders and you don't want the distraction. It was important to show up and turn the page and start fresh. And be as positive as I can."

All this is not surprising, if you trace Luongo's roots. His parents, Antonio and Pasqualina, were strict. An Italian immigrant who relocated to Montreal in 1979, Antonio constructed and delivered furniture. Pasqualina worked in marketing with Air Canada.

"When I was a young teenager, my dad used to bring me to work with him on weekends," says Luongo.

"I'd work for a furniture company and then he had a shoe store and I'd try to sell shoes—even if I was the shyest kid ever. It was not an easy job. My dad to this day is still working and so is my mom, even though I've told them many times that they can stop. He's over 50 now and still carrying pieces of furniture on his back and that shows you what kind of person he is.

"It's all about the work ethic. No matter what your situation is, you've got to work and my dad is a perfect example of that."

So is his son.

ADAMS AWARD
Engraving includes Quinn and Vigneault

PAT QUINN AND ALAIN VIGNEAULT moved to the front of the class among Canucks coaches when they became recipients of the Jack Adams Award.

The Adams Award is the plum award for coaches because it recognizes the NHL coach deemed to have contributed the most to his team's success, in much the same spirit as Adams, whose dedication was legendary.

"Pat and Alain are very much alike when it comes to having a really good feel for their people, whether on or off the ice," says Ryan Walter, who played for Quinn and coached with Vigneault. "It's no coincidence that they're both highly respected among their players and peers."

The consistency of their approach, each and every working day, caught the attention of Steve Tambellini, an NHL player in Vancouver and later a Canucks executive, who worked alongside both men during his tenure on the West Coast.

"They know what they want, they tell you what they want and will give you a chance to do it," Tambellini recalls. "There is no wavering and that's why people enjoy working with Pat and Alain."

The steadfast Quinn became the first Canucks coach to be honoured with the Adams in 1992, when he directed Vancouver to first place in the Smythe Division with a 42-26-12 record for 96 points. Two years later, the Canucks would reach

Above: Pat Quinn was an imposing figure behind the Canucks bench, where his coaching ability included forming a lasting trust with his players.

Left: An obviously pleased Canucks coach Alain Vigneault graciously accepts the Jack Adams Award that evaded him earlier in his career when he called the shots from the Montreal Canadiens bench.

Some words of wisdom from coach Vigneault in the heat of battle to young Canucks players Ryan Kesler (left) and Mason Raymond.

the Stanley Cup Final for the second time in franchise history, with Quinn still calling the shots.

The sometimes stubborn Irishman also doubled as general manager in those days. The previous year, in 1991, he had had the task of replacing head coach Bob McCammon when the team was underachieving. Quinn picked himself as replacement and the rest is history.

The Canucks were 11 games below .500 during the 1990-91 season when Quinn reluctantly dismissed McCammon, a close friend since their days in Philadelphia when they played for the Flyers.

Quinn made his move when he decided the Canucks needed an injection of new blood. He went behind the bench and, at the trade deadline,

was proactive when he pulled the trigger on two major deals that netted five new faces, along with a refreshing attitude.

The Canucks acquired Geoff Courtnall, Cliff Ronning, Sergio Momesso and Robert Dirk from the St. Louis Blues for Garth Butcher and Dan Quinn.

The second deal saw Dana Murzyn join the Canucks from the Calgary Flames for Ron Stern and Kevan Guy.

Vancouver missed the playoffs in the spring of 1991, but the stage had been set for a quick getaway when the next season began. Quinn got the Canucks out of the starting gate with an 8-1-1 record—and that was before scoring sensation Pavel Bure arrived in November.

"They know what they want, they tell you what they want and will give you a chance to do it."

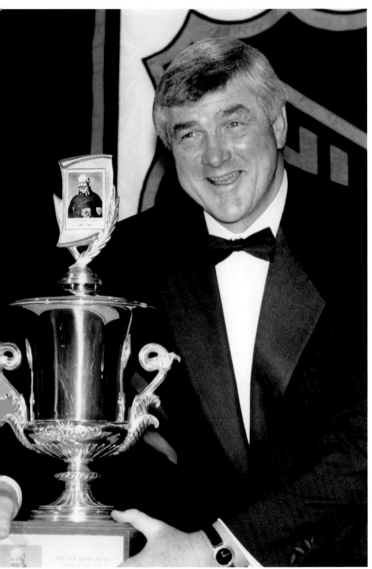

Quinn was all smiles that brilliant June day in 1992 when he accepted the Adams Trophy as the NHL's coach of the year.

Quinn also appointed young Trevor Linden as team captain and the Canucks asserted their will-power in becoming a playoff contender.

"The timing was incredibly right for what the Canucks needed," says Tambellini. "Players trusted Pat, that Pat would always do the right thing, not only for the team, but for the individual. He had a wonderful relationship with his players."

Seven players scored 20 or more goals in 1991–92, with Linden, Bure and Adams reaching the 30-goal plateau. In addition, netminder Kirk McLean set a club record with 38 wins in 65 appearances.

The Canucks won their division by scoring 44 more goals than in the previous season, and allowing an amazing 65 fewer. Plus, the fans were having fun again at the Pacific Coliseum as Quinn championed a style of play that was pleasing to watch and support.

Vancouver was the buzz of the NHL at the time and Quinn was duly rewarded for his efforts, by being selected Adams winner over finalist Roger Neilson of the New York Rangers.

"I strongly believe Pat Quinn never got enough credit for what he did,"says Courtnall, who scored an overtime goal for the Canucks in the fifth game of the 1994 playoff matchup against the Calgary Flames. "Pat was a great, great coach. He knew when to come down on guys and when to give other guys room to grow. I don't think many guys could have coached our group of players the way he did."

Quinn set the bar for coaching in Vancouver, a standard that would not be reached until the Canucks hired Alain Vigneault for the 2006–07 campaign, after he guided the Manitoba Moose in the American Hockey League during the previous season, developing Vancouver's top prospects in the minors, including Alex Burrows.

In a three-day period in June, with the NHL draft in Vancouver, Canucks general manager

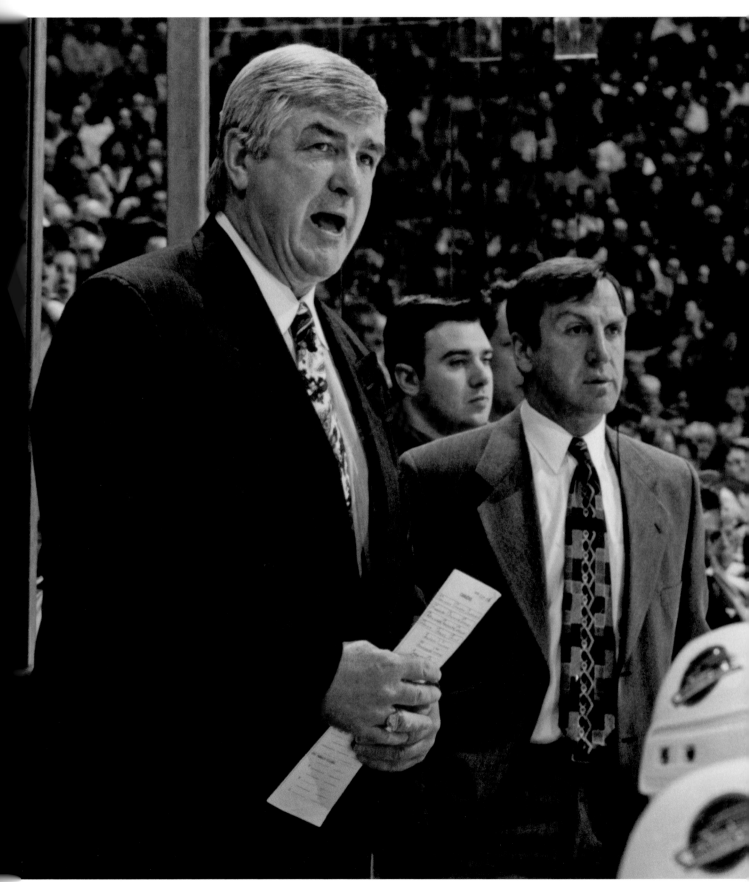

With lineup card in hand, Quinn barks orders as assistant coach Stan Smyl and trainer Mike Burnstein have their eyes glued to the action.

Dave Nonis hired Vigneault for his second NHL coaching stint and traded for goaltender Roberto Luongo. Once again, the stage had been set for improvement.

"Management knew this about Alain—his messaging was very clear," Tambellini says. "If there's a problem, he's dealing with it right now. He's consistent that way.

"Some say he's an emotional coach, but he's one of the most poised coaches around. He's a passionate man, but at the same time he's steady in approach. And, he has a way of confronting his best players to make them better. That is a true talent in the NHL."

Vigneault found that life as a head coach in a major Canadian market can be a daunting task with the internal pressure to win and the external attention and daily banter about your team with the amassed media throng covering one of "Canada's teams."

He had been tested as a young coach at age 35 when he was appointed head coach of the storied Montreal Canadiens in 1997. The training provided AV (as media call him) with the ability to laugh at himself and deal with the daily routine using his unique sense of humour.

He once pronounced, while standing at the podium during his daily de-briefing, "It 'tis, what it 'tis," before bursting into hysterics.

In his first Vancouver season, Vigneault helped the Canucks establish a club record with a 49-win season, followed by two rounds in the playoffs. The Canucks were a mediocre team at the Christmas break, then won in Calgary on Boxing Day and were off to the races. Vancouver lost just seven times in its final 35 games before the playoffs and finished 49–26–7 for 105 points, the most in club history. Luongo won 47 times in goal, while the Sedins, twins Daniel and Henrik, established themselves as offensive leaders.

NHL broadcasters selected Vigneault for the 2007 Adams Award ahead of Lindy Ruff of the Buffalo Sabres. It was a satisfying moment for Vigneault, after being runner-up to Joel Quenneville of the St. Louis Blues in the 2000 voting when Vigneault coached Montreal.

TREVOR LINDEN
Tears of endearment

ONE OF THE MOST MEMORABLE nights in Vancouver Canucks history had little to do with a game, which says something about both Trevor Linden and the franchise he helped transform.

Linden failed to bring a Stanley Cup to Vancouver—getting closest in Game 7 of the 1994 Stanley Cup Final—and yet somehow still exceeded expectations, while becoming the heart and conscience of the Canucks for nearly 20 years.

All that he had done, all the traits Linden represented that we all wished we possessed, were revealed in a dam-burst of emotions on the epic night of April 5, 2008.

If we can agree that there will probably never be another Canuck whose impact on his community was as deep and transcendent as Linden's, then we must know that there will never be another night like that one.

It was Linden's final game and by the time it ended—after the numerous unscripted standing ovations, the Calgary Flames' receiving line and a prolonged lap of honour by the winger from Medicine Hat to say both thanks and goodbye—there was hardly a dry eye in the Canucks' house.

About six hours earlier, the only one crying was Linden.

"I'd leave my house every day around 10 minutes to four, quarter to four, to go to the rink," Linden explains. "My wife, Cristina, was usually at

Above: Linden's intensity illustrates a player that was considered the heart and soul of the Canucks.

Left: About to gather speed, there would be no stopping the swooping Trevor Linden when he was in high gear as captain of the Canucks.

work. But as I was walking out the gate, she just pulled up. She came home early to see me go. Immediately, when I saw her—and I'm a lot like my mom, I hold my emotions in—as soon as I saw her I started to cry. She knew what that was all about.

"As I was driving to the rink, I knew it was my last time. I was flooded with memories and emotions, thinking, 'This is my last game.' I'm sitting there in my suit, driving to the rink, stopped at a light and I'm crying. Some guy was looking at me through the window, like, 'What's wrong with you?'"

Linden's grit and determination in the greasy areas pays off with a goal against the Phoenix Coyotes.

So, if you happened to be between Kitsilano and General Motors Place about 4 p.m. on April 5, 2008, and remember seeing a tall guy in a GMC Yukon blubbering like a Miss America winner, relax, it was only the greatest Canuck savouring his final day on the job.

"Once I got to the rink, I was fine," Linden continues. "Before every game, around 4 p.m., I would sit with Henrik and Daniel [Sedin], and Mattias [Ohlund] would show up about 10 minutes later. We'd sit in the players' lounge and watch other games going on in the East, and we'd talk and have coffee. I used to bug the twins because they'd always want to watch Detroit with all the Swedes. We'd talk soccer, talk hockey. Then you start getting into game mode.

"I think it probably crossed their minds, but no one was going to say, 'Hey, is this your last game?' But, absolutely, I was thinking, 'This is the last time I'll ever do my skates up for a game.'"

Some people were already crying during the warmup, holding signs thanking Linden, telling him he was loved—not that there was much doubt—and that he'd be missed.

Canucks coach Alain Vigneault, his team eliminated a few days earlier from the playoff race, started the 37-year-old with the Sedins on the first line. But it was when the trio came out for the third period faceoff that things really began to get emotional. Linden was leaning on his stick, focussing on not crying and wondering why the heck no one was dropping the puck.

When he looked up, he was alone. Centres Henrik Sedin and Craig Conroy had backed out of the faceoff circle. Everyone had, except Linden, leaving him in the spotlight. Neither he nor his team was very good that night, losing 7–1. It hardly mattered.

The performance for which Linden is best remembered was that colossal Game 7 on June 14, 1994. He scored both goals in a 3–2 loss to the New York Rangers. The bell tolled for Vancouver when Nathan LaFayette's shot rang off Mike Richter's goal post in the final minutes.

"When I think back to that day," Linden says, "I remember trying to get some sleep in the afternoon and just having my eyes glued to the ceiling, thinking, 'Boy, we're one game away from carrying the Stanley Cup around Madison Square Garden.'

"I think for hockey fans in B.C., that's probably the game I'm most identified with. I had a history of performing well in big games, so people identify me with Game 7 of the Stanley Cup Final. I think I've played better games than that, for sure. But perception is reality."

There was no confusing perception or reality nearly 14 years later on Linden's final night.

Anyone who witnessed it knew instantly that this would never occur again—not to this degree, not with such raw emotion from all sides.

Eight months later, Linden's No. 16 was retired and lifted to the rafters alongside mentor Stan Smyl's No. 12. That was another emotional night, but planned. "A funeral without the tragedy," Trevor's brother Dean called retirement.

Linden is genuinely at a loss to explain the strength of the connection fans felt toward him. Pressed for an answer, he stammers, "I've always been a guy who tried to work hard and do what's right." At his retirement ceremony, he asked people to remember him simply as someone who had the time of his life playing a game he loved.

He knew, that April evening in 2008, what was ending. So did everyone else.

"When I think of the people who have had Hall-of-Fame careers in all the sports, a guy like Joe Sakic, who's a good friend and an amazing player—he never got a last game like I did," Linden says. "There's not a lot of players in any sport who have had that kind of farewell. It's not lost on me. I'm incredibly lucky."

Fighting back tears, Linden takes his final bow on April 5, 2008, as the adoring crowd stands as one.

LUONGO'S DAY
On golden pond

BEING A CREATURE OF HABIT, especially on game days, Roberto Luongo had to drastically change his routine during the 2010 Olympic Winter Games. Evening games are the norm for most NHL teams, but Team Canada was not assigned a single evening start at Canada Hockey Place.

Usually, during the NHL regular season, Luongo would participate in the morning skate with Canucks teammates at 10:30 so that he could get a feel for the situation. He'd take shots, review defensive strategy with coaches, go home for a meal, be with his family and rest for a few hours before an evening start time.

Not on February 28, though. Luongo's day had a much different feel to it, starting with an early breakfast in the Olympic Village with Canadian teammates as they prepared for the championship game against the United States.

Start time was high noon, about the time Luongo would normally be leaving the dressing room for home during the regular NHL season. Not this time. A world-wide audience would be tuning in for the much anticipated gold medal game, a rematch of finalists from 2002.

"I had to alter my approach to things, but at the end of the day it's always mind over matter," Luongo says. "Sometimes you just have to be ready to change your ways. This time I didn't have too much time to think about the game. It was

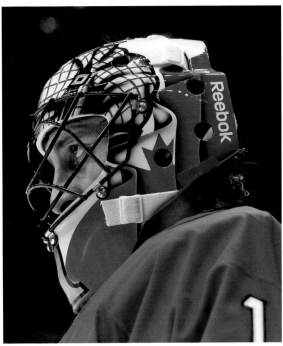

Above: Luongo's ability to adapt to change allowed the Canucks goaltender to earn a gold medal with the Canadian men's hockey team at the 2010 Olympic Winter Games.

Left: A victory lap to be cherished forever in the life of Roberto Luongo as the goaltender in Canada's electrifying gold medal Olympic overtime victory that held an entire nation in suspense on the afternoon of February 28, 2010.

breakfast, come to the rink early and be ready to go. I was able to keep the nerves down a little bit more than if it had been a night game."

Luongo did manage to find time to phone his wife, Gina, who was host to family and friends in Vancouver while Roberto was housed at the Olympic Village.

Olympic men's hockey medallists were honoured on March 13 when the Canucks played their first home game following the 2010 Winter Games. Gold medallist Roberto Luongo of the Canucks is flanked by silver medallist Ryan Kesler of the United States (left) and bronze medallists for Finland Jarkko Ruutu (Ottawa Senators) and Sami Salo (right). Canucks staffers Mike Burnstein and Pat O'Neill also toiled for Canada.

"I think she might have been a little more nervous than I was," he says. "It was stressful for my whole family. It might be easier to play than watch in these situations. Everyone was so excited, but she remembered to give me the one piece of advice she gives before every game: 'Don't get hurt.' She worries about my safety."

Luongo got to the rink about 9:30 that morning and remembers his Canadian teammates being quiet for the most part. Sticks were massaged and taped, equipment was checked, and the mood generally was one of silent confidence, knowing that a hockey-crazed nation would analyze their every move once players hit the ice.

"You could tell by the quietness that guys were excited to get the game started," recalls Luongo. "Not much was said before the game, no big speeches or anything like that, maybe because it was the biggest game of our lives. It was electric in the room even though it was pretty quiet.

"Before the warmup, [head coach] Mike [Babcock] came in briefly. He said a few things that I really don't recall. But I do remember him before the overtime, saying that we should go out

there and have fun because this is what we play hockey for. He said something like, 'Somebody in this locker room is going to be a hero. It's just a matter of finding out who it's going to be.'"

Everyone remembers Canadian star Sidney Crosby wearing the hero's mantle after his overtime goal against U.S. netminder Ryan Miller. What some people forget is that Luongo made a huge arm save on American forward Joe Pavelski just moments before Crosby converted a pass from Jarome Iginla at 7:04 of the sudden-death overtime.

"I only had a few shots in overtime and it was a spin move by him—I just reacted," says Luongo. "I got a piece of it with my elbow. I was going to freeze it and end the play, but I let the puck go and we ended up going to the other end and scoring.

"It's amazing, really. Who knows what would have happened if I had just frozen the puck."

Instead, a few seconds later, the exuberant Luongo raced out of his net toward Crosby and teammates at the other end of the rink, raising his arms high over his head in celebration and thanking the hockey gods in the way he knows best.

"I got a piece of it with my elbow. I was going to freeze it and end the play, but I let the puck go and we ended up going to the other end and scoring."

"You work your whole life for something like that," he says. "It was a feeling that I will never forget, a special moment in my life. I was happy I was able to have that in Vancouver.

"The intensity all game was unbelievable. I was getting 'Looooo' all game by the fans. You could tell they were excited, but just as nervous as we were."

Luongo's personal cheering section included his mother, father and brothers, his wife and in-laws, making it, "A great family time, too."

As for his equipment, it didn't go missing after the game, as Crosby's stick and gloves did. Luongo probably has Canucks equipment manager Pat O'Neill and his staff to thank for that. Luongo wore his goal pads and blocker glove in practice for the rest of the season, keeping his stick, mask, catching glove—and gold medal—for his personal collection, or for possible donation to the Hockey Hall of Fame.

Luongo's amazing Olympic journey left him grateful for the once-in-a-lifetime opportunity to play in front of the country and Vancouver fans at the same time.

"The way things unfolded, replacing Marty Brodeur in the playoff round, taking over and being able to win in front of our fans in overtime, with my family in the crowd, it was just so special," Luongo adds. "Just tell everyone I'm thankful."

Roberto Luongo makes another key save for Canada in the gold-medal game of the Olympics, denying Paul Stastny of the United States.

HENRIK SEDIN
Two League trophies say it all

IT TOOK DECADES OF BLOOD, sweat and sometimes tears, but the wait was well worth it—all 40 years— thanks to Henrik Sedin. The Vancouver Canucks slick-as-silk centreman from northern Sweden had a season for the ages in 2009-10.

The passer turned scorer accomplished what no other Canuck had ever done when he won the Art Ross Trophy as the NHL's leading scorer, then added the prestigious Hart Trophy as the player judged most valuable to his team. And, believe it or not, he did it without having twin brother Daniel at his side for nearly a quarter of the games.

Henrik took it all in stride, of course, suggesting at the Las Vegas awards ceremony that the Canucks were still missing the trophy that matters most, the Stanley Cup playoff championship. Team comes first with the Sedins.

"That's the trophy we're missing," says Henrik. "I think we're really postured to go forward."

It was only a few years ago the Sedins were portrayed by critics as being too slow afoot to be hugely successful on North American rinks.

How could they possibly be productive offensively when not having breakaway speed to score off the rush?

Well, a decade later, Henrik—Hank to teammates and friends—has two major awards on his resume after setting a Canucks team record with 112 points. The brothers reached star status also

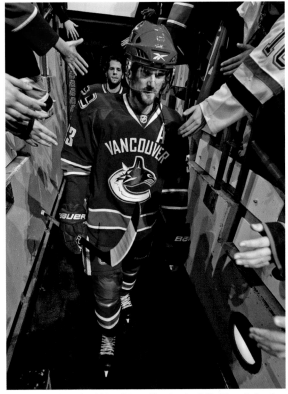

Above: Henrik Sedin found himself in good hands as he thrilled Canucks fans in 2009-10 on his way to winning the Art Ross Trophy as the NHL's leading point producer, and the Hart Trophy as the league's MVP—a first for Vancouver.

Left: Henrik Sedin took to shooting the puck more during the 2009-10 season and the Canucks reaped the benefits when the centreman scored 29 times, the most in his career.

when Henrik was named to the NHL First All-Star Team and left-winger Daniel to the Second Team.

The red-heads imported from Örnsköldsvik have met expectations, and then some.

Brothers Henrik (33) and Daniel (22) Sedin are an imposing sight when they move into the offensive zone to create scoring chances from their nifty passing.

The Sedins' road to stardom took many twists and turns, including an early realization that they needed to improve their physical strength before they could get faster and best use their God-given playmaking talents.

The brothers readily admit that they weren't where they needed to be physically. So in the summers, back home in Sweden and away from the constant surveillance of Vancouver media, Henrik and Daniel trained like never before.

"We didn't want to be average physically," Henrik says. "We wanted to be among the best. We wanted to come back every year in top shape."

When they were in their mid-teens, the Sedins didn't train specifically for hockey in their off-seasons. They were elite soccer players, with Henrik chosen for the Swedish under-17 national team. Daniel wasn't selected, partly because he was moved out of mid-field and away from Henrik to an unfamiliar flanking position. That summer they decided to focus more on hockey, working to catch up physically with their puck-playing countrymen.

When they reached the NHL, though, the Sedins found they needed to become even stronger, not just for their puck-protection game on the cycle in the offensive zone, but for the explosive skating needed to enter the offensive zone.

Being competitive with each other helped in their transformation. They competed in training, always trying to out-do each other. They had learned the value of competing and pushing each other from older brothers Stefan and Peter, whom they idolized as youngsters.

Henrik and Daniel made huge strides with their strength and skating. By their sixth NHL season they were deemed point-a-game players. They learned how to handle the day-to-day routine of the NHL, balancing the game with their families and training routines.

In the summers, the Sedins changed their workout routine to accommodate their families. The brothers are married—Henrik to Johanna, Daniel to Marinette—with children to command their spare time. So they altered their schedules. Instead of two workouts a day, morning and late

Henrik Sedin came home with an armful of NHL awards in 2010 when he earned the Art Ross Trophy (left) for the scoring title and the prestigious Hart Memorial Trophy as the league's most valuable player.

"Hank had always had the ability to score, but maybe the injury to Danny allowed Hank to become more comfortable in the dirty areas around the net. He began to think 'shoot' a lot more."

afternoon, they went to one session, a condensed four- or five-hour push for improvement.

The benefits were noticeable, critics conceded, as the Sedins got quicker and held the puck longer. They were stronger and went to the net more frequently. Now the team leaders offensively, Henrik and Daniel were given the prime time they so richly deserved.

Still, there was always a nagging question posed about the Sedins. Could they play proficiently without each other? After all, they had been hockey line-mates since Daniel moved to the wing when they were 12 years old.

The Canucks discovered the answer early in the 2009-10 campaign when Daniel suffered a

broken bone in his foot in the fourth game of the season. He was hit by a booming slap shot launched by teammate Alexander Edler. Daniel would miss the next 18 games, leaving Henrik to fend for himself.

"With Danny out, Hank seemed to gain more confidence in himself," says teammate Kevin Bieksa. "Hank had always had the ability to score, but maybe the injury to Danny allowed Hank to become more comfortable in the dirty areas around the net. He began to think 'shoot' a lot more."

Daniel had always been the shooter and Henrik the passer when the Sedins worked their magical mystery tours in the offensive zone. Now it was Henrik who would alter his game in order to

Henrik Sedin begins one of his patented rushes with a look of determination that has become part of his trademark in the NHL.

Henrik Sedin takes a breather on the Canucks bench while head coach Alain Vigneault decides whether it's time to again unleash the NHL's most productive playmaker.

produce enough offence for the Canucks to get by during Daniel's absence.

"At first it wasn't a lot of fun because we enjoy playing with each other," Henrik recalls. "I knew there was going to be more pressure. If I had gone four games without scoring, people would have said, 'He can't play without Daniel.'"

Henrik didn't score right away, but his game elevated. He took more shots, eventually scoring twice against Detroit and three times on Colorado. In the 18 games without his brother, Henrik produced 10 goals and eight assists, a point a game on average.

"People told me throughout my career I needed to shoot more," he said. "But nobody really told me that when Daniel was out. I think it just came naturally."

So, no one was more pleased with Henrik's increased scoring than his brother. "He obviously wanted to prove to everybody that he could do it without me," says Daniel. "By doing that, he had a lot of confidence. Once he knew he could play without me, he kept playing that way when I got back. He kept going to the scoring areas. He's not on the outside so much and takes pucks to the net. Improving by 30 points is really remarkable."

The evolution of Henrik as a complete player continued throughout the season. Daniel returned to the lineup November 22 and the brothers resumed their dominating play. Henrik finished the season with a career-high 29 goals and a club record 83 assists for 112 points, a 30-point increase.

His assists were one more than his point total the previous season.

Daniel also produced 29 goals, in only 63 games. The durable Henrik played all 82 in the regular season for the fifth consecutive year. They both averaged better than 1.3 points a game as they moved into the company of elite NHL offensive players.

"The capping of the evolution goes with Hank's attention to detail," Canucks assistant coach Ryan Walter says. "Now he gets the puck more than ever, starting with his improvement on faceoffs. Also the Sedins don't cycle as much anymore. They use that shuttle play where they go from the side boards inside to the net. They've adapted some little pieces that allow them to play closer to the net."

Frequent linemate Alexandre Burrows observed that Henrik was more sure of himself from the start of training camp. "You could tell he was going to make more high-risk plays no matter where he was on the ice. I admire him because he's always been a positive guy that goes about his business. Even if he hasn't scored for a few games, he stays the same and keeps working hard."

Henrik answered any doubters by proving one of the brothers could be successful without the other. He told a close friend it was an important time for both. No matter who was out of the lineup, it was up to the other to carry the torch.

Then he added, with a wink: "We can do this with each other, too."

PHOTO CREDITS

All photos courtesy of the Vancouver Canucks' photo archives, unless otherwise noted below.

Front jacket photo, Vancouver Canucks / Andi Mortenson
Back jacket photo of Kirk McLean and Trevor Linden, Vancouver Canucks Archive / Credit Unknown